May 9, 1989

to Wythe,

It has been an absolute
delight getting to know you
these past months. You
are a very special lady —
don't ever forget how
beautiful you are — inside
& outside — with love
Gabe

"There is only one happiness in life—to love and be loved."
—George Sand

Love and Be Loved

LOVE & BE LOVED

Making Love the Most Wonderful
Experience in Life

John A. Tamiazzo, Ph.D.

REVISED EDITION

TRANSPERSONAL PSYCHOLOGY
RESEARCH & EDUCATION PRESS
P.O. BOX 91339
SANTA BARBARA, CALIFORNIA 93190-1339

LIBRARY OF CONGRESS CATALOGING-IN-PUBLICATION DATA Tamiazzo, John A.
    Love & be loved.
    Reprint. Originally published: North Hollywood, Calif.: Newcastle Pub. Co., 1986.
    Bibliography: p.
    1. Interpersonal relations.   2. Love.   3. Self-actualization (Psychology)
    I. Title.   II. Title: Love and be loved.
[HM132.T358   1989]   302.3'4   88-29599
ISBN 0-9621459-0-4

Published by Transpersonal Psychology
   Research and Education Press
Post Office Box 91339
Santa Barbara, CA 93190-1339

"Each one of us was created to love and be loved"
—*Mother Teresa*

CONTENTS

INTRODUCTION

CHAPTER I   LETTING GO 3

CHAPTER II   CHANGE 19

CHAPTER III   OPENING TO LOVE 29

CHAPTER IV   TRUST 61

CHAPTER V   UNCONDITIONAL LOVE 71

CHAPTER VI   AWAKENING THE HEART 83

CHAPTER VII   MAKING LOVE THE MOST
               WONDERFUL EXPERIENCE
               IN LIFE 101

CHAPTER VIII   WRITE A NEW SCRIPT 109

CHAPTER IX   LOVE IS FORGIVING 119

CHAPTER X   50 WAYS TO LOVE AND
               BE LOVED 132

REFERENCE BIBLIOGRAPHY 137

ABOUT THE AUTHOR 139

INTRODUCTION

Sometime ago I was invited to speak at one of the local colleges on the subject of self-esteem. One of my first questions to the class was, "What does it mean to have healthy self-esteem?" One young man said, "It means that you trust yourself." Another responded, "It means that you like yourself." A third person said, 'It means that you are kind to yourself, respect and accept yourself."

My second question to the group was, "What do you think interferes with liking, trusting, and respecting ourselves?" The responses were, "Thinking that you aren't as good as others; criticizing yourself, punishing yourself, being afraid to try something new and do things differently!"

My third question to the group was, "Where did you learn to treat yourself with disrespect, mistrust, and unkindness?" One girl said, "From my family. I never was treated with respect at home. I was constantly told how not to feel or how I should feel." Another response was, "I came from a very mistrustful household and I learned about being mistrustful from my parents. They told me over and over again, don't trust people. I remember when I got into some trouble with a friend and they told me how disappointed they were wth me. They would never trust me again!" A young woman said, "My mother told me in so many different ways that I was a real burden to her. Dad left us when I was very young and it was really difficult being given so many responsibilities at such an early age. It seemed that I couldn't do anything right. Mom was a heavy drinker and when she got drunk, she also got very abusive with me. I grew up believing that I was the worst daughter in the world!"

As we continued our discussion, one young lady said, "I just can't compete with the women in Cosmopolitan Magazine! I don't look like a model, I don't have the money to buy expensive clothes, I am not five foot eight, nor do I have a body that even slightly resembles theirs!" One young man said, "I'm really a nice guy. But I don't look like any of those guys on the soaps! I don't have an M.B.A., I'm not a therapist, and I don't drive a BMW. I don't belong to Nautilus either!"

We have so many culturally imposed standards of how we should feel, what we should wear, what we should look like, the life style we should be living. If there is one major block to self-esteem that we could identify it would be, 'comparing ourselves to others whom we believe are more successful, smarter, more attractive, luckier, more creative and gifted.' Of course there are things or talents that others have that we may not have but there are also talents we have that another person does not have. When we compare ourselves to others, whether we think we are better or worse off, it only serves to diminish who and what we are. It only prevents us from really discovering the wealth of creativity and beauty that lies dormant within us.

A story from my own life will provide a good example. Years ago when I first began my career as a counselor in psychiatric hospitals, I wanted to be the best I could be. But one very significant person was stopping me from realizing my true potential. His name was Fred. No matter what I achieved, no matter how many outstanding programs I organized, no matter how much research I did in the field of psychology, Fred always proved to be the better, the smarter, more articulate, more creative, more attractive. As far as I was concerned, he was a much more vibrant person and skilled therapist than I. One night we decided to get together and have a few drinks and get to know each other better outside of the hospital setting. After a few drinks I turned to Fred and confessed, "You know something. I have always wanted to be more like you! I really respect who and what you are and the great work you do!" Fred looked at me and said, "You know something. I have always wanted to be more like you! I have the deepest respect for your ability to conceive of an idea and then to carry it out." It was at that point that we became very good friends.

The fact is, we admire people because they mirror something deep within us that wants to be released. I didn't look like Fred and couldn't look like him; there would be no point in trying because I look the way I do and he looks the way he looks. But, there was a way he expressed himself that really impressed me; there was a clarity in his thinking, a strength in his convictions. These were the qualities I admired in him, these were the qualities I proceeded to more deeply explore and express in my work and in my life. To simply compare myself to someone else and to think that I am less or inferior is terribly destructive. But to see that person I so deeply respect is an important teacher for me and represents an unexpressed part of me is a very creative and constructive attitude. It wasn't until we had that conversation together that this truth was revealed to me. But, the other fascinating thing is the discovery that I too was an important teacher for him. I was able to do things he wished he could do. We all have that ability and we all are teachers for one another, whether we want to believe it or not. Each one of us has many gifts to share. Each one of us has a well-spring within of ideas, goals, talents, abilities, creativity, joy, and love. We are full, yet oftentimes we feel so empty. We are courageous, yet oftentimes we are so afraid. We are so wise, yet oftentimes we forget all that we know. The pendulum swings both ways; it's just a part of our humanness. Let it swing . . . move with it, flow with it and allow all that is you to be expressed. Embrace and accept the beautiful person that you are.

This is a book about pathways to love. There are many for us to explore, and all of them will contribute to opening our hearts to loving and being loved. Each pathway represents a door for us to open and walk through, a bridge to cross, a lesson from which to learn and to grow.

Love and Be Loved

. . . . . When love is guiding and influencing
your lives
They will be full and abundant and will
be fulfilled
When each person can truly find that
spirit of oneness
Whether it is in a home
A group
A community
A nation
A world
Then there will indeed be peace
Peace within
And therefore that peace will be reflected
without
and will manifest itself by peace for the
whole
But it has to start somewhere
Therefore let it start within you as the
individual
And so grow
From that tiny spark within
To a mighty blaze without.

Eileen Caddy
Foundations of Findhorn

CHAPTER I

LETTING GO

Love is often a problem.

Why is the most beautiful, sacred, and incredibly wonderful experience in the world a problem? How did love become a problem? It isn't a problem when we are 'in love' and we have that 'special person' in our lives. Love certainly doesn't seem to be a problem then. As a matter of fact, it is marvelous!

But how about when we don't have that special kind of love relationship and relating? Is love a problem then? What happens when the romance doesn't seem to be there anymore, or when our partner seems disinterested, pre-occupied, aloof and always busy doing 'something else'? When does love and loving turn into a problem instead of a joyous and fulfilling experience? When do we come to that point of frustration and say, "I've invested enough in this relationship and I just can't give anymore!" When do we give up on love because we have been disappointed too many times? When do we stop risking?

If we believe that we are victims of giving and loving, and it seems like we aren't receiving anything in return, we need to take a serious look at what/why/how we are giving: the messages we are communicating, the needs we are trying to fill and have filled, what unsettled past experiences we may be re-creating in our current relationships. Learning what it means to 'give' is one of our most important lessons. As we become honest with ourselves, begin looking within instead of without and are clearer about our wants and needs, we are on the path to healing ourselves and our relationships.

The following is a vignette from a discussion which took place during one of my workshops.

First Person: "I'm tired of being the one who is always on the giving end of the relationship. There are a lot of 'takers' out there who are sapping me of my energy. I am tired of giving and giving and not getting anything in return!"

Second Person: "I used to feel the same way as you, but I came to see that I was attracting that 'needy' kind of person into my life because there was a part of me that wanted to experience being deprived. In this way, I held onto my resentment from the past and blamed the other person for all the misgivings in the relationship. Therefore, I didn't have to work on myself and could point to the other person who needed to change. I didn't have to take responsibility. I formed so-called 'one-way' relationships because I didn't believe I deserved better. But the fact is, I didn't know any better. This was the kind of relationship I was familiar with and used to and so I just lived with the frustration and disappointment. It was better than being alone."

The key to really loving and being loved, then, is a process of 'letting go' of the past experiences, beliefs, attitudes and negative inner messages we have come to associate with love and being loved. Some of us have been deeply hurt, abandoned, lied to and mistreated. Some of us have been raised in emotionally wrenching home environments and our childhood memories of love are filled with pain and disappointment. Some of us had parents who just weren't there for us emotionally and physically. Some of us are so discouraged about the meaning of love that we aren't sure we can really open up and trust again.

When we hold onto a painful past and cling to the unhappy memories of childhood, our present and future will reflect more of the same. 'Letting go' is learning to be receptive to what we can do *now*, how we can change *now*, what direction we can take *now*. Often we get sidetracked and continue to suffer and punish ourselves for what we did, what they did, the way we were, what we could have done and should have done, rather than having the confidence to trust in our ability to change, to grow, to explore, to discover, to create, to love and be loved.

In 'letting go,' then, we are courageously accepting the responsibility for breaking the unhealthy patterns of love and loving we learned from the adults who served as our role models. One of the ways we perpetuate old habits of relating is to blame 'them' for our current problems or life style. Blame will get us nowhere. Instead, we need to take a serious look at how the patterns began; for the fact is, our parents taught us what they learned from their parents and relatives and on and on it goes. We are part of the family chain.

How did we learn about love? This learning includes, but is not limited to, our observations of our parents, what we perceived, the body language we became familiar with, the facial expressions, mannerisms, the consistencies and inconsistencies, what we were told was acceptable and unacceptable behavior, how safe we felt at home, the words we heard, the way feelings were expressed; in short, the whole rhythm, pulse and spirit of the home environment. So we need to ask ourselves and reflect upon some very important questions in regard to what we learned about love and expressing love from mom, dad and all the significant adults from our past who were our teachers.

How did you see them express their love toward each other? Were mom and dad respectful toward one another? Toward us? Affectionate? Kind? Did they have a good sense of humor? Were they supportive, encouraging, controlling, domineering?

How demonstrative were they? Do you remember a lot of hugging, touching, kissing, embracing?

Did your parents' eyes communicate love? Anger?

How available were they to you? Did they talk to you? Ask you how you felt, or what you needed?

Did you really feel loved or did you usually feel you were a burden, in the way, unimportant? Were you afraid of them or did you feel safe? Did you feel understood?

What words did you learn to associate with love?

After an argument, how readily did your parents forgive one another? Did they hold onto their anger/resentment for a long time?

Was there a lot of giving and sharing at home? Did the family spend time together?

Was there a lot of anxiety and confusion at home?

Was love withdrawn when you were bad or when you didn't meet their expectations of you?

Did you feel like you had to constantly please and appease them to win their love, affection, and attention?

What loving traits do you associate with your father? What loving traits do you associate with your mother?

What did you learn about how men relate to women from your father? What did you learn about how women relate to men from your mother?

Did you learn that it is okay to make mistakes?

Do you want to have a relationship like your parents?

What are the important lessons about intimacy you learned from them?

'Letting go' is a process of slowly uncovering our early family dynamics and committing ourselves instead to expressing the healthy, positive aspects of our nature. We don't have to continue living out an unhappy and unfulfilled adulthood because our childhood was that way. We don't have to continue the unhealthy patterns of love and loving with our own children, spouses, partners, family, or friends. We can break the family chain and free ourselves from the habits, values, perceptions, beliefs and ways of interacting with which we imprison ourselves, but only if we choose to. The past is to learn from, not to get stuck in.

'Letting go' is learning to have the confidence and to trust in our ability to change, to grow, to explore, to discover all we are capable of, to create, to love and be loved. For many of us, this isn't going to be easy. It takes time to undo and unlearn the unhealthy habits and unfulfilling life scripts which we inadvertently learned. It takes time to let go of beliefs which no longer serve a purpose and to let go of the attitudes which prevent us from experiencing a more joyful life.

'Letting go' is the willingness to release the roles and self-concepts in which we are stuck and attached. Like the first speaker in the workshop dialogue I quoted earlier, many of us over identify with being the 'victim,' the 'loser,' the 'guilty one,' the 'unloved one,' the 'successful one,' the 'poor one,' the 'lonely one.' The more strongly we identify with a particular concept of self, the more strongly we have established our limitations. As Ram Dass and Paul Gorman have written:

> Important in any model of who we think we are is the message to everyone about who they are. It's not as if there are any real secrets. If we are only seeing one part of the picture about ourselves, positive or negative, that's all we'll be able to make real to anybody else. Caught in the models of the separate self, then, we end up diminishing one another. The more you think of yourself as the 'therapist'; the more pressure there is for someone to be a 'patient.' The more you identify as a 'philanthropist' the more compelled someone feels to be a 'supplicant.' The more you see yourself as a 'helper,' the more need for people to play the passive 'helped.' You are buying into, even juicing

up, precisely what people suffering want to be rid of: limitations, dependency, helplessness, separateness. And that's happening largely because of self-image.

If we learned early enough to unconsciously associate love with pain, disappointment and loneliness, we may not even realize that we are re-creating those early family dynamics in our current relationships again and again. Therefore, if we hold tenaciously to the belief that we have been hurt in love and will be hurt again, we mentally identify all the people we meet as untrustworthy and potential 'heartbreakers.' We have already determined that intimacy, openness and trust will inevitably lead to disappointment and to being hurt again.

'Letting go' is a commitment we renew everyday to awaken and to express our uniqueness, creativeness, inner beauty and unlimited potential. At this moment you may not feel particularly creative, beautiful or loving. The problem is in your perception of yourself and your past and current circumstances, the places you have been looking for love and the situations you have been drawing to yourself. We make choices every moment of our lives—healthy ones and unhealthy ones. It may not seem like we choose our pain, but the fact is we choose the attitude we hold at any given time. How we use our time and energy is all important. We can use it for any purpose we choose. We can use our energy to create havoc in our lives and we can use it to heal ourselves. To heal is to make whole, to correct our perception of how we see ourselves and others. How can we begin the healing process if we are constantly limiting our potential and that of others?

We need to be using our time and energy to learn how to love ourselves and to accept the love of others. If we continue to use our time and energy to live in fear and frustration, we will see others as having the power to harm us and our little world will get smaller and smaller. If we are constantly worrying and apprehensive about the worst, the darkest, the saddest and most tragic, our fears will probably come true. We create and become what our mind dwells upon. If we spend all our time obsessed about illness, losing our money, our job, our relationship, our sanity, the world blowing up and people finding out what a terrible or uninteresting person we believe we are, then life will painfully pass us by. If we use our time to be resentful, angry, vindictive, fault-finding, and guilty we will only go around and around in circles attracting what we fear and dislike most, never getting what we really want: to love and to be loved.

Love is a creative power, continually discovering new forms of expression. When we are really loving we aren't in pain, we aren't blaming the world for our suffering and dissatisfaction, we aren't so filled with fear and guilt that we are unable to move. When we are extending our love we are expressing the deepest, fullest, and most joyful and powerful energy within us. We are extending our very essence. This extension is 'letting go.'

Learning to love and be loved is being receptive to all the outer and inner resources we have available to us. Inwardly we are very rich. The belief in our own inner poverty is an unhealthy and addictive way of seeing ourselves and the world as lacking, deficient, inadequate and incomplete. We have been taught that to be fulfilled is to be successful in the outer world: to own a dozen cars, live in a palace, buy beautiful clothing, have a face lift, a nose job and have all the niceties of life. But unless we have a sense of purpose and meaning, a deep respect and love for ourselves, we will never feel rich and full inside and know what it means to live joyfully. There may be many parts of ourselves that we want to change, many qualities that we want to free ourselves of, but we must also maintain an inner regard for the many positive qualities we already possess.

The ancient Delphic oracle 'Know Thyself' is as important for us today as it was thousands of years ago. The more intimately we know ourselves the more we know about love because we come to discover that our very essence is love. The more we extend that love, the more love will fill our lives. Not a clinging love or a love fueled by guilt, pain or fear, but a love that expands, encourages, enriches, enlivens and heals.

As we reach out to others in life, in friendship or service, offering our assistance wherever it is needed, we learn about the unlimited powers of love. In our unity lies our strength, in our respect for each other's uniqueness lies our peace of mind.

Learning to love and be loved is learning to share our beliefs, feelings, concerns, fears, insights, discoveries and experiences. Sometimes the parts we share are painful. Sometimes we may feel that we have nothing to share at all. At times looking within and honestly facing ourselves is not easy. We are often afraid of what we will find down there. We are often afraid of really knowing who we are and what we want. But we must share the feelings no matter how difficult it may be. Share with a friend, a counselor, a support group, but share. No matter what we are going through or how difficult and confusing life may be at this time, we can pick up the pieces and move ahead. All the experiences from the past are there for us to learn from.

Some of us learn our lessons very slowly; some of us learn quickly. Sometimes it seems that we aren't learning a thing. All that really matters is that we begin. That we let our guard down for awhile and slowly chip away at the attitudes, beliefs and false self-concepts separating us from ourselves and others. There is a beautiful and loving person deep inside us, buried beneath all the roles, expectations, tapes and memories of the past. We have just forgotten.

Learning to love and be loved is a process of healing ourselves and our relationships. For many of us loving has been 'conditional' and the very conditions we live by are the blocks and barriers to love. Love has no conditions. It is, in itself, unconditional. We need to free ourselves from the 'I would love you more if . . .' conditions. The 'if only you would just . . . every thing would be ok' beliefs. The 'I love you when . . .' attitudes. To love unconditionally is to simply say, "I love you."

'I love you' is an attitude, it is a way we relate, it is reflected in our thoughtfulness, our mutual respect, our trust and our responsiveness to encouraging one another. 'I love you' means I care about you, your welfare, and I am here to help you in any way I can.

Somewhere in life we learned that if 'they' change, or 'you' change, things will get better. This is the illusion many of us get stuck in. The fact is, the change needs to begin in us. Unconditional love means removing the 'shoulds' and the 'if onlys' from our thinking and vocabulary; discarding the 'if I had done . . . things would be better' tapes from our faulty belief system. Whenever we place conditions on ourselves we place the same limitations on others. The 'if only I had' inner tapes are translated into 'if only you would' attitudes and all we've done is place the responsibility and problem elsewhere. Why are we so afraid to look within?

What are we risking when we begin to really take responsibility for ourselves? Are we afraid to change because we fear the response or disapproval of our partners, parents, or friends. Are we afraid of making a mistake? Are we afraid of losing the relationship? Life may seem humdrum but at least it's familiar, manageable and we know what to expect. But we also need to ask ourselves if we are using these relationships as an excuse for avoiding taking responsibility and risks.

A friend of mine was really beginning to question what she wanted to do at this point in her life. She knew she needed to be more creative, and she decided to go back to school. Her husband was not the least bit encouraging and didn't seem to approve of her decision because it was taking too much time away from their relationship. He was very successful and totally involved in his career but he wouldn't support her in working toward her own success and fulfillment. Obviously, her decision created a lot of disharmony at home. But, she feels she has to follow what she knows in her heart is the right course for her, and if each of them is willing, together they can work on resolving whatever feelings, fears, conflicts or concerns arise.

In all our relationships, we have the opportunity to encourage each other in discovering the ability to create, to love, to work and enjoy life. This is the basis of friendship. Often times we forget to be friends to each other in our so-called most 'intimate relationships.' Unless we remember to do this, we will never grow spiritually together, but rather grow slowly apart. Our personal growth is intricately connected to our commitment to help those we love in any way we can, to share whatever we have to share, to encourage each other to live full and creative lives.

It's very important to communicate our needs to our partner: our needs for intimacy, for affection, for sharing and for expressing ourselves in new and creative ways. Sometimes the communication is very threatening. When two people have been relating in the same way for such a long time 'change' becomes a dangerous word. It becomes a threat to the predictability of the relationship. But change is essential to growth and to learning what we are capable of becoming. When our basic needs for self-discovery, creative expression and love are not acknowledged, or are denied by fear of the disapproval of another, we and our relationship with that person are slowly dying.

Learning to love and be loved means not trying so hard, trying to relax more, seeing the absurdity of our melodrama and cultivating the ability to laugh at ourselves. It means to lighten up, to be more spontaneous, not to take ourselves and our lives so damn seriously. There is a time to be serious and to put forth effort and a time to let things flow, to 'let it be.' Like nature, our life has seasons.

We learned about our inalienable right to the pursuit of happiness in school, but if we are always pursuing happiness and not taking the time to enjoy and be happy in the present moment, our sense of joy will always seem to lie in tomorrow's conquest, or in tomorrow's achievement. 'Letting go' is opening ourselves to the day we have before us—to this very moment.

Learning to love and be loved is opening to the Spiritual dimension of our being. It is a process of learning how to become inwardly quiet and to gain trust in a Higher Will or Inner Spiritual Guidance. Meditation can be most helpful in this process, and it can also be helpful in loosening our grip on the unhealthy patterns we want to change and in freeing us from the self-defeating emotions that seem so often to be in control.

Learning to love and be loved means learning to know ourselves at the deepest level, to become good friends with ourselves, to care for and nurture our own inner needs, personal growth, health and peace of mind. Love is freedom. Love is learning what it means to give, opening our hearts to forgiveness, trust and our own unlimited potential. Learning to love is the journey to our inner truth and the Oneness we share with others.

Some of my greatest teachers have been children. Their innocence, spontaneity, curiosity, recuperative powers, playfulness and wisdom are qualities we all still have but which most of us have lost sight of. If our childhood was unhappy or if, due to family circumstances, we had to act very adult when we were a small child, that inner child remains within us buried beneath the fear, mistrust, and built up resentment from the past. Rediscovering and awakening the child within is one of the most exciting experiences in this process of 'letting go' and opening the door to that loving energy inside.

A lovely friend of mine shared her daughter's poetry with

me as I was working on this chapter and it was so beautiful
I want to share it with you. Barbie wrote this when she was
ten. Eleven years later she was killed in an automobile
accident, but she has left us with these insightful and
sensitive impressions captured when she was ten.

> Love is a sundrop touched by a lonely hand.
> Bringing two people together
> Like doves flying off into the sun
> Their slim and graceful bodies twisting in the air
> That sundrop is the miracle of life....

Once there lived a village of creatures along the bottom of a great crystal river. . . . Each creature in its own manner clung tightly to the twigs and rocks of the river bottom, for clinging was their way of life, and resisting the current what each had learned from birth. But one creature said at last, I am tired of clinging! I trust that the current knows where it is going. I shall let go and let it take me where it will. . . . And taking a breath he did let go and at once was tumbled and smashed by the current across the rocks. Yet in time, as the creature refused to cling again, the current lifted him free from the bottom and he was bruised and hurt no more. The river delights to lift us free, if only we dare let go. Our true work is this voyage, this adventure.

Richard Bach
Illusions

CHAPTER II

CHANGE

Change is vital to life. As a matter of fact, change is life. Without change life becomes stagnant, dull and very predictable. Change opens doors to possibilities we haven't even dreamed of yet.

Change affects every aspect of life. We change jobs, change careers, change relationships, change where we live, change the car we drive, change our appearance, change our attitude, change our mind, ad infinitum. Oftentimes change or the thought of change brings about a lot of anxiety and all sorts of fears associated with losing what we have; losing what we are familiar with. For many of us, venturing into the unknown isn't easy. We, therefore, are often very resistent to making changes and 'letting go' of what we have for fear of making a mistake, a miscalculation, or ending up with something worse.

The fact is, change can be very exciting if we view it as a transition and a natural process of inner growth and development . . . a process of transformation. It's one thing to change the car we drive and quite another to change the very core of our life; to change our attitude toward ourselves, others and the world around us. Transformation means changing our perception of how we see ourselves and expanding our awareness of what we are capable of doing . . . of increasing and stretching the possibilities and choices for making life exciting and very fulfilling.

The process of transformation has always fascinated me as I have explored and observed the changes within my own life and within the thousands of lives of those I have had the opportunity to work with and to know. I have found that there are identifiable stages or phases which are not necessarily linear, but rather circular, meaning that we experience the phases again and again. Sometimes the changes involved are rather simple and occur very easily and naturally. Sometimes the changes are very complex, difficult, and seem to be overwhelming. Oftentimes the most significant changes are within our own belief system. We make an attitudinal shift in how we interact with others and suddenly 'see' ourselves in a whole new light. Life opens up to us in ways it appeared to be obstructed. What seemed impossible now seems attainable. What we were once afraid of no longer has the power to stop us from doing what we know in our heart we must do. Transformation, then, is a metamorphosis.

The first stage or phase is a period of gaining a deeper awareness of how we have been limiting ourselves by what we think and believe to be true. If our negative self-concept is that 'we are not enough,' then we will probably remain 'stuck' and settle for a lot less than we really want and are capable of. If we want to love and be loved, yet we believe that 'we aren't lovable' or that 'love is too painful,' then we will probably spend much of our life alone or in an unfulfilling relationship wishing and hoping things were different but refusing to make the changes and attitudinal shifts which will open the doors to love. Our thoughts create our reality; our thoughts create the life we live today and the life we will live tomorrow; "our thoughts," as Stephen Levine once wrote, "are our karma."

The second phase begins our inner work. During this time we may find ourselves searching more, reading more, wanting to learn more about who we are and what we are capable of. We may take a class, join a weekly support group, join a club, study our dreams, see a counselor, attend seminars, travel; the possibilities are endless. The whole purpose of the second stage is self-discovery; to learn more about what we want and how to get it.

This can be a very difficult period. One woman I know experienced a deep sadness when she realized how lost she had been. "What have I been doing with my life?" she asked. "Where have I been all these years?" The fact is, most of us have been living through so many facades, roles, and expectations of how it could have been or what we should have done that when we finally begin to poke holes in what we thought we were and in what we thought we wanted, we often experience anger, grief and guilt. This transition is difficult enough without the added burden of guilt. This guilt represents an inner resistance to change. Our ego is very devious and vindictive. There is a healthy part of us that wants to change and live a fuller life and there is an unhealthy part of us that wants to remain stuck with anger, resentment, and guilt and keep life the way it is. Being aware of this inner struggle is very important.

The healthy part is the understanding that we no longer have to live in the past, that even though we experienced a deprived childhood doesn't mean we have to experience an unhappy adulthood. Because the past was riddled with unpleasant memories doesn't mean that life today can't be a wonderfully fulfilling experience. We can make a new choice, but we have to be willing to let go of the struggle and the beliefs that no longer serve a constructive purpose.

The healthy part of us may be a faint voice that gives us hope and encourages us on. Oftentimes it is overpowered by mother's voice, father's words, a critical phrase, an old tape which discourages us over and over again. The healthy part of us still has faith and trust and wants so much to trust again. It is the part of us that wants to be at peace with ourselves and our world. It is the part of us that wants to speak up for what we believe in but has been afraid to take the risk. How deeply we are committed to listening to and to following the guidance of our healthy inner voice will ultimately determine our success with this second phase. Our commitment to the process of self discovery is all important. Our commitment and dedication to making our life a joyous adventure begins right now.

The third phase is a period of sorting out. We begin to see more clearly as to what we want and no longer want. It is a time of 'letting go" of all the roles and negative self concepts we have gotten stuck in. It is a period of makng decisions, making choices, and testing out our wings. "What about my life do I want to be different?" "What about myself do I want to change?" "What is no longer working and no longer a source of joy and fulfillment?" "What would I love to do (even though I might be afraid) at this particular junction in my life?"

One very important part of this phase of change is to pinpoint the sources of stress in our lives. People who are high achievers know how to effectively handle stress. Becoming aware of the early warning signs of stress; difficulty sleeping, feeling tired often, restlessness, easily aggitated, tension, depression, health problems, and poor eating habits, to name a few, helps us to see the need for change. Illness can often be viewed as a resistance to making necessary changes in life. When we are under a lot of stress we are involved in an inner struggle; resisting a part of us that wants to be expressed, listened to, and understood. Illness can be viewed as a warning sign that we are denying ourself something that is essential to our psychological and spiritual growth. Denial takes many forms, but the most important opportunities we will discover we are denying ourself are the experiences of really loving and being loved.

Self-acceptance is one of the 'keys' to this phase and the process of 'letting go.' Acceptance means that we will work on breaking the habit of judging, criticizing, or comparing oursevles to anyone else. The fact is, no one is less than or more than we we are; no one is better or worse; we are one and each person we meet is our teacher in some very special way and we are theirs. Acceptance means that we will stop blaming ourself for the things we've done in the past, stop blaming others for the hurts they've inflicted on us. This doesn't mean we are going to deny what happened. It does mean that we are going to face our feelings. Acceptance means that I no longer have anything to hide and I accept responsibility for my own life. It is an affirmation: "I love myself, I have renewed faith in myself and trust in my abilities to do whatever I choose to do; I respect who and what I am. My continued growth and welfare are my top priority. I have the right and freedom to experience joy, health, prosperity, and inner peace." The sincerity of our commitment to this change of attitude is all important.

The fourth phase opens the channels to our imagination. So often creativity is assumed to be the domain of artists, musicians, dancers and writers, whereas creativity really represents an optimistic attitude and constructive approach to life. When we are living creatively we do work that we love, our relationhips are fulfilling, and we believe in ourselves. When we are living creatively, we know we make a difference and we have cultivated the ability to enjoy life, accept challenges, take risks, and try things we have always wanted to try but didn't take the time. To live creatively means that we have learned how to 'brainstorm' in virtually every situation we encounter. This means we are able to see many possibilities, options, and ways of solving a particular problem or concern, rather than feeling 'locked in' or limited. The only thing which limits us is the restraint we place on our imagination.

Our imagination is one of our greatest resources. It is the inner power to vividly 'see' our successes before we actually take any specific action. No matter what we want to achieve or succeed at, the power of our imagination to make it a reality and to open the doors to prosperity and abundance in all areas of life is absolutely essential.

The ability to visualize how we want our life to unfold is really the first step toward success of any particular goal. It is a power we all have available to us, a power which can help us move beyond and through any obstacle if we will take the time to open the channels to this magnificent resource. One of the problems we often have is believing that the universe will not provide. It is what I call a 'scarcity consciousness.' It is the belief and 'inner movie' that we don't deserve to live a full and vibrant life and that we just aren't capable of making it a reality. It is the belief that life has not been good to us and that we are on the planet to just get by. If this is the belief and visualization that we are creating again and again, how can we possibly expect anything different? In order to make significant changes in how life unfolds, we have to change the way we see it; we have to take the time to visually create abundance and prosperity instead of lack; we have to take the time to use the creative power of our imagination to open the doors to loving and being loved.

The fifth phase represents a dedication and commitment to opening our heart and mind to others more and more; to open to life itself. We know about the power of imagery and use it. We've discovered the wisdom of appreciating ourselves and others and communicating positive thoughts and words. We know how to handle rejection and have cultivated a positive attitude toward our 'so called' failures; we learn from them and make the necessary changes and proceed. We are self-validating and know how to take good care of ourselves. In other words, we have become very good friends with ourselves. This commitment to love and to maintain a positive attitude will help to improve all our interpersonal relationships and make life rewarding instead of a constant struggle, disappointment and daily routine.

The important thing is to take the risk. It doesn't matter what the circumstances are. What matters is how important we believe we are and how important it is for us to make changes which will open the doors to experiencing a more honest and fulfilling life; to take the next step rather than 'waiting' for something to happen.

I remember seeing a newspaper cartoon wherein a couple were both sitting side by side in bed reading. He was reading a book titled, "How To Communicate With Your Wife," and she was reading a book titled, "How To Communicate With Your Husband." They were both lost in their own little world. I wonder how long they were going to read before they actually took the next step . . . to put the information to good use?

"Is there a special way to avoid pain?"
"Yes, there is a way . . . . .
Look at every path closely and deliberately.
Try it as many times as you think necessary.
Then ask yourself and yourself alone one question. . . .
Does this path have a heart?
If it does, the path is good.
If it doesn't, it is of no use. . . .
One makes for a joyful journey; as long as you follow it,
you are one with it.
The other will make you curse your life.
One makes you strong.
The other weakens you.

Carlos Castaneda
The Teachings of Don Juan

CHAPTER III

OPENING TO LOVE

I remember reading an excellent article in *Writer's Digest* entitled, "Conquering the Ultimate Writer's Block." It was the author's conviction that the stronger and more deeply we believe in, and trust in, ourselves and our abilities, the more absolute our success. Talent, perseverence and dedication are all essential, but if at a deeper level we really don't believe in and fully trust ourselves, we are likely *not* to succeed. He listed some of the most common negative inner messages held by writers who remain unpublished:

1. I don't have the self-discipline
2. I don't know anything about people
3. Editors won't like my stories
4. Rejection would destroy me
5. I don't have enough talent
6. I have nothing to say to people

7. I have boring ideas
8. Nobody wants to listen to me

Much of the same could be said of overcoming the obstacles that prevent us from loving and being loved, of "Conquering the Ultimate blocks to Love," if you will. How many of us believe, at the deepest level, that we aren't lovable, or that if we fall in love it will end in a disaster? How many of us believe that if we were rejected by another we would be crushed? How many of us believe that we aren't enough as we are and live with the ache of being alone because of what we anticipate the consequences of a relationship will be? How many of us don't do the things we know in our heart we want to do for fear of another's disapproval or judgement?

If our childhood is riddled with disappointing and hurtful experiences and we haven't worked through and 'let go' of our resentment, then our past will continue to determine our present and future experiences. Our past can help us see ourselves and our lives more clearly today or it can continue to cloud our vision.

The painful memories, hurts, disappointments and negative inner messages we hold onto from the past create our reality today and our future reality. They become the foundation of our belief system: what we believe, what we are left with, what we associate love with, what and who we think we are. If mom and dad weren't demonstrative and never touched, held, kissed, embraced or spoke loving words to each other, if they seemed to live in their own separate worlds even though they lived in the same house, then these will be the guidelines by which we will form our relationships. These are the patterns we will tend to recreate. We also learn about love and self-esteem from our peers, significant family members, our religious training, t.v., books, soap operas, and from the hypnotic lyrics of songs. If we are repeatedly humming, "I'm nothing without you baby," this is what we are programming ourself to believe.

Our past experiences, then are the seeds from which our beliefs and attitudes about ourselves and the meaning of love sprout. They become like programs in the brain's bio-computer. These tapes play over and over again in our heads, "I'm guilty," "I'm unlovable," I'm stupid," "I can't trust," "I've got to prove my worth." They are lived out in our interactions with others, in the way we feel about ourselves and in the way we approach and live our lives. Guilt, blame, fear, resentment and all the other feelings we refuse to let go of need to be seen for what they are: as barriers to love and being loved.

Rejection won't destroy us, but our response to being rejected can. Rejection doesn't feel good; it can really knock the wind out of you. But we'll be able to breathe again, form loving, harmonious relationships, if we can begin to see where our experiences of, and attitude toward, rejection began.

Sometimes we don't want to see, don't want to let go of the pain and resentment, don't want to let go of the little world we lived in long ago and continue to live in. I remember a woman telling me about all the unfulfilled relationships she had experienced. For her, it was one rejection after another. She came to the conclusion that all men were jerks and couldn't be trusted. She told me there wasn't a friend she had whose relationship with a man she was the least bit envious of. I asked her about her relationship with her father. It had sounded to me like there was a lot of unfinished business between them, a lot of painful and disappointing memories. She told me that there was *no* problem with her relationship with her dad. He was always drunk, rude, unavailable and obnoxious! She didn't want to discuss it any further.

How can we love and be loved when we feel so guilty or are so overwhelmed with fear that we can't trust ourselves or anyone else? How much fear is standing in our way to really living and enjoying our lives? How do we let it go? How do we develop nurturing and creative attitudes when we already feel overwhelmed by life?

You don't need to answer these questions right now, just become aware of the attitudes about yourself you possess at this time. Attitudes are learned and can be unlearned if we are willing to make the changes and open the doors to seeing ourselves in a new and healthier way. We often stand in our own way, clinging to, and refusing to let go of, the very traits and habits that are making our lives miserable and blocking us from the life for which we really yearn.

There are ways to overcome the obstacles within us, ways of living life that are saner and healthier and more wholesome than those we practice now. They are not difficult, they only require commitment and patience with oneself and one's inevitable lapses along the way.

Let's take a look at some of the things that seem to stand most often in the way of our loving and being loved, learn what we can about their origins and what steps we can take to overcome and free ourselves from them.

When we were children many of us were told by parents

or teachers that we were 'bad,' a 'problem,' or were causing them a lot of 'heart aches.' Do you remember hearing any of these?

"How can you act like that when . . ."

"Why can't you be more like your brother (or sister)?"

"You'll be sorry when I die!"

"I thought you loved me! How could you have done that?"

"I will never trust you again! You have really disappointed me!"

These are guilt messages. Their intent is to make others do what the speaker wants them to do by making them feel guilty and ashamed of their actions. Anytime we feel we have acted incompetently, hurt another or failed in winning another's approval, the response is guilt. Guilt may be one of the most prevalent emotional torments we experience. Its pervasiveness makes it difficult to pin down and to attach to any particular event or circumstance. Many of us are saturated in guilt and in what we did or didn't do; and these feelings seem to seep out through our pores affecting virtually every aspect of our lives.

Guilt is also a means of avoiding taking any corrective steps. Instead of doing anything about the unhappiness we experience, we merely feel guilty and then continue the same pattern again and again. Wayne Dyer writes:

> "Guilt is not merely a concern with the past; it is a present moment immobilization about a past event. And the degree of immobilization can run from mild upset to severe depression. If you are simply learning from your past, and

vowing to avoid the repetition of some specific behavior, this is not guilt. You experience guilt only when you are prevented from taking action now as a result of having behaved in a certain way previously. Learning from your mistakes is healthy and a necessary part of growth. Guilt is unhealthy because you are ineffectively using your energy in the present feeling hurt, upset, and depressed about a historical happening. And it's futile as well as unhealthy. No amount of guilt can ever undo anything."

GUILT is a difficult emotion to let go of because it is our learned response to the feeling that we have done something wrong or have 'sinned' in some way. We learned about feeling guilty when we were very young. We learned it at home, in school and from our formalized religious training. Guilt is an insidious form of self-hatred and self-imposed limitation on how happy and loved we believe we deserve to be. It is the way we have learned to punish ourselves to avoid being punished by someone or something else. This illusion, expecting to be punished, is the very energy which fuels our guilt over and over again. Often we believe that experiencing guilt is necessary so that we can be forgiven for all the things we should have done differently. There are a lot of 'shoulds' attached to feeling guilty. "I should have been more understanding," "I should not have caused them so much trouble," I should have been more honest," "I should have never been born!"

What are the crimes and unforgiveable mistakes you made that you refuse to let go. What are some of the things you did that you still feel guilty about? What "should you have done differently"? How many 'shoulds' do you use to 'should upon' yourself?

Guilt can be exhausting and is one of the major sources of illness, pain, confusion, addiction and self-pity. At times I've compared guilt to a one act play masterfully performed again and again. In the drama we assume all of the roles; judge, jury, prosecuting attorney and defendant. The supporting cast may change, but the scenario and outcome are always the same; our ego defense gets stronger and is more cleverly executed but the verdict remains the same . . . guilty. And who continues to create this drama? We do. And who is the only person who can let us off the hook? We are.

The fact is, we did what we did and our parents did what they did. We did the best we could have done with the knowledge and understanding we had at the time. Our parents did the best they could have done with the knowledge and understanding they had at the time. We cannot change the past but we can change what we hold onto from the past. The present is all we have. The present is our only reality.

In the book, "In Tune with the Infinite," Ralph Waldo Trine wrote:

> "When we come fully to realize the great fact that all evil and error and sin with all their consequent sufferings come through ignorance, then wherever we see a manifestation of these in whatever form, if our hearts are right, we will have compassion and sympathy for the one in whom we see them. Compassion will then change itself into love, and love will manifest itself in kindly service. Such is the divine method. . . . and one becomes a true master to the degree that the knowledge of the divinity of his own nature dawns

upon his inner consciousness and so brings him to a knowledge of higher laws; and in no way can we so effectually hasten this dawning in the inner consciousness of another, as by showing forth the divinity within ourselves simply by the way we live."

Our unfinished issues with our past, then, are intricately connected to our feelings of guilt. Guilt is a predicament that we can do something about if we are willing to see it differently; if we are willing to view it from a new and healthier perspective. To begin freeing ourselves from guilt, we need to:

1. *Become aware of the guilt laden messages and tapes we are holding onto and believe to be true.* We learned them from the situations of the past and may be perpetuating the self-same patterns in our relations with our own children, spouse friends, and family members. Take the time to search out the old tapes that are still part of your vocabulary and belief system.

2. *Take inventory of all the mistakes, wrong doing, unkind acts and words you feel responsible for and guilty over.* Remember you cannot change the past, but you can change what you hold onto from the past and what you believe to be true. If there are things you did and are ashamed of, make a commitment not to make the same mistake again, but by all means, don't expect perfection from yourself. This is where a support group, counselor or friend you can share with, and trust, is so vital to the process of healing. They can help reinforce and strengthen your commitment. Know your needs and weaknesses, ask for and seek help if you need it.

3. *Remember that you learned to feel guilty when you were very young in response to the belief that you caused your*

parents and others grief and pain; and these negative self-concepts and beliefs were reinforced over time.

4. *Open yourself to the pain and suffering from the past.* When we feel guilty we are in pain and need to embrace our humanness. Denying our guilt feelings and projecting them onto someone else will ultimately only reinforce our feeling of guilt. We need to face what we feel and share those feelings with another.

5. *Know that guilt is perpetuated by our thoughts, attitudes and self-concepts.* We can let go of guilt if we choose to and when we are ready. We learned it, we've chosen to cling to it, we can let it go.

6. *Recognize that we have been deeply hurt and that our anger and resentment over what 'they' did or didn't do also leads to further feelings of guilt.* We often suppress our anger because we feel guilty for feeling angry at being hurt. In other words, our feelings take us around in circles. It is important to find constructive releases for our pent up emotions: running, sports activities, yelling, screaming, digging, pounding, laughing, crying, etc. When I'm angry, oftentimes I yell at myself in the mirror then stop and stare and yell again. Sometimes I look so ridiculous that I begin to laugh. It's a great release and a way to 'let go.'

7. *We must always keep in mind that anger is never the real problem and continue working to uncover the under-lying hurt, pain and sadness that lie beneath.* We get angry because no matter what we seem to be accomplishing in the outer world, our inner world is not being nourished and attended to. In a sense, anger is a response to the feeling that we are not really living but are just getting by or sur-viving. It is a deep inner frustration with feeling unable to

express the depth of our potential. It is the feeling of power-lessness in not standing up for ourselves and in what we believe in.

8. *Recognize that our parents' frustration with their own lives was often expressed as anger toward us.* Most of the things they accused us of, and blamed us for, were a pro-jection of their own pain. Their patterns were in turn learned from their parents and were all unknowingly passed down to us. In many cases, we became the targets of their own self-hatred and dissatisfaction with life. Who is the target of your own frustration with yourself and your life?

9. *See guilt as a way we punish ourselves again and again.* Why are we holding onto our guilt feelings? What purpose is guilt serving us now? How long are we going to cling to what we did or didn't do or could have done differently?

10. *Know that guilt and love cannot co-exist.* One negates the other. Love is our very essence; not guilt, not sin, not evil, not jealousy or fear. These are all barriers to love's presence.

11. Let go of the erroneous believe that guilt is natural and that if we didn't experience guilt we would harm others. Experiencing guilt won't stop us from hurting another, but love will. Somewhere along the way we learned that the sociopathic personality doesn't experience guilt and this accounts, in part, for their inability to stop hurting others again and again. Guilt isn't going to prevent one's attack on another; only love will do that. Love is what joins us together; guilt only serves to separate and isolate.

12. *Open our heart to the spiritual dimension of our be-ing.* For some people, praying to a saint, spiritual teacher or to God brings about an inner feeling of peace. For some, meditating on uplifting words/affirmations/thoughts/im-

ages or the teachings of a Spiritual Master brings about an inner stillness and clarity. For some, being one with nature and experiencing a cosmic or universal awareness is the source of inspiration and joy. For some, dedicating their life to a project which helps humanity in some very important way brings about a sense of fulfillment and purpose. For some, regularly attending a group whose goal is spiritual enlightenment can bring life into balance. The important thing is to find the spiritual pathway, activity, philosophy or discipline which is right for you and dedicate yourself to it. By "right" I simply mean one in which your involvement, participation and experience brings about an inner sense of peace, a deepened understanding, a sense of purpose and meaning and a feeling of connectedness to others.

The key to opening to the spiritual realm is surrender. 'Surrender' means that we recognize and accept that we are part of something much greater than ourself; that there is a universal and Creative Power always accessible to us; that there is a Higher Will which must take precedence over out little egos' will; that we can let go of the struggle and open our hearts to the wisdom that there is a better and more fulfilling way to live. 'Surrender' means we become more receptive to the values, attitudes, aspirations, priorities, choices and power of love (which join us together for the highest good of all concerned).

When we surrender, we have taken a most important step toward letting go of guilt. As we learn to ask for the inner guidance we seem unable to give to ourselves, for the direction we seem unable to find; as we begin to tap and trust our intuition and to begin to understand the meaning and wisdom of loving ourselves unconditionally; we find we are embarking on the path to freeing ourselves from the power we have given to the voice of guilt, anger, resentment and the past.

13. *Learn what forgiveness means.* To forgive is to let go, to free ourselves and others from the limitations and misperceptions by which we have been guiding our lives. Forgiveness is the most powerful lesson we have yet to learn; for to forgive is to make peace with ourselves, to see the past with greater clarity, a deeper and richer understanding and as a stepping stone to move ahead with our lives.

14. *Know that the awareness of the things we do, say and hold onto is the first step in healing ourselves and our relationships.* Letting go of the feelings we no longer want is a commitment we need to renew every day.

BLAME is one of the most common responses to feeling helpless, impotent, disregarded and unfairly treated. We blame mom and dad for not laying a good foundation for us and accuse them of being responsible for the way we are and all the problems we are experiencing. We blame our spouse or partner for the difficulties which exist in our relationship. We blame karma for all the misfortunes and painful circumstances we seem to attract. We blame God for abandoning us, punishing us and not giving us a full deck to play with.

We search and look everywhere for reasons and rationalizations to justify our anger, bitterness, jealousy and scorn. But we need not look far. The choices we make, the beliefs about ourselves we cling to, the values we live by, the priorities we establish either contribute to our personal inner growth and spiritual development or hinder it. To blame another or the world or even ourselves is one of those choices.

To believe ourselves victims is to believe that the past will repeat itself again and again, and we have no choice in the matter. To believe ourselves victims means that we are holding onto the unpleasant memories and situations of the past. Letting go of the role of 'victim' means releasing ourselves from these obsessions and taking responsibility for the direction of our lives *now*; in the decisions and choices we can make *now*.

It is important to recognize how much pain a person is in when they constantly blame and criticize others. Their blaming is a cry for help and a call for love. Unfortunately, when we are the target of another's anger and frustration, we usually don't realize this or care. All we know is that we are being attacked and our response is to defend ourselves from the onslaught. We may say something to put the other person in their place. We may return the attack by criticizing them. We may walk out. But if we want to move on to a healthier lifestyle, at some point in our lives we have to realize that blame is the expression of a past hurt which has never been healed. One of the greatest tragedies of human interaction is not seeing beyond another's anger and blaming to the call for love and that lies within.

Blame is also a method (though an ineffective one) many of us use to gain control of our circumstances when we feel helpless and vulnerable. The need to feel in control of our circumstances is a big factor when we feel overwhelmed with life. If it is *your fault*, that lets me off the hook (at least temporarily). But inwardly we know the truth! We really need to take hold of our lives, but we're not at all sure what it means or how to do it.

Blame is a self-imposed trap because we chose to see our situation as a problem instead of as an opportunity to learn and grow. Some have described a feeling of *being stuck, helpless* or *in a rut*: When we get into these moods we may react bitterly and angrily and strike out at everyone, particularly our spouse, partner, parents, God and whomever we feel emotionally connected to.

How do we get trapped? We get trapped in our thoughts, in past memories which were unpleasant, beliefs which we accepted as true, old attitudes, responses and habits. When we feel trapped we are identifying with our limitations, with what we don't have or what we think we are lacking. We get stuck in angry feelings about 'what happened when,' about what 'they' did or didn't do, about what we were denied in our childhood, about what happened last year or last month.

The fact is, we were hurt in the past. We need to face this, allow ourselves to experience the pain again, then release it and let it go. This doesn't necessarily happen in one week, one month, or even one year. But the process can begin for you right *now*. For as long as you are still holding onto the angry and negative feelings of the past, you are allowing them to eat away at your better self and letting their impact on your life and the lives of others deepen and spread.

Sometimes a so-called 'tragedy' is the pathway to our spiritual evolution and transformation. The tragedy, the accident, the divorce, the unexpected move, the loss, the separation, the disappointment, the sudden change in circumstances can all be motivating factors that allow us to tap inner resources we never knew we had. If we didn't experience difficulties, we wouldn't learn anything.

Our lessons aren't always easy; sometimes we wonder: "Why is this happening to me? Is there anybody up there?" Every problem we experience is an opportunity for us to learn, to receive all the riches life has to offer. We can do things we never dreamed possible.

I remember reading a wonderful story about a Chinese family. The father bought his son a white horse and all the neighbors marveled at its beauty. They told the father how lucky the young lad was to own such a regal animal. One day when the boy was riding he fell off and broke his leg. It was a very serious break and the boy was bedridden for many months. The neighbors told the father what a tragedy that he had broken his leg. If only the young man hadn't owned the horse, they said, the accident would never have happened. Shortly after a war broke out and all the able-bodied young men were summoned to leave their homes to fight in the war. Now the neighbors told the injured boy's father what good fortune it was that his son had broken his leg, since he would be spared going to war and being killed. Following the boy's recovery his horse ran away and the boy became very sad. The neighbors told the father what a tragedy it was that the horse the young man loved so dearly had run away. All through these months the father had never regarded these situations as being tragic but, rather, had seen them as the way of things. He knew in his heart that everything would be fine because he believed in the sacredness of life. And one day the white horse returned but not alone. A dozen or more majestic horses had joined her and now the family had more horses than they ever dreamed of. And the neighbors told the father what good fortune it was that the mare had run away; for she brought so many horses back with her. (Wouldn't it be wonderful to have this much faith in life?)

After one of my lectures I was approached by a young woman who told me the following story. She had been an active person who joined the Peace Corps to help teach English in the jungles of South America. After spending a year there, she contacted a rare disease. Now she had to have blood transfusions every month or so just to stay alive. It was an incredibly difficult situation to adjust to emotionally and physically. But because of this so-called 'tragedy,' she developed an appreciation for life that she never thought possible. Everyday she was facing the prospect of death, but she was also facing the prospect of life, depending on how she chose to view it. For her, every day was a gift to be lived fully, courageously and lovingly.

This woman was working on a counseling credential and wanted to help others to really 'see' the preciousness of life. People were already seeking her out to discuss problems they were experiencing. She wanted to help them but hesitated because she wasn't officially a counselor yet. I told her that her energy, stamina, radiance, and love for the sacredness of life was an inspiration to everyone who had the opportunity to talk to her and be in her presence. I told her to listen to what her heart told her and follow its guidance. She beamed with joy and thanked me. I thanked her in return for all she had shared with me during that hour.

Often we forget about the gifts we carry within no matter what circumstances surround us. The young woman could have easily given up and succumbed to the tragedy of her accident. She could have blamed everyone, including herself for having gone into the jungles in the first place. Instead, she choose to live life fully and joyfully, seeing every day as an opportunity to learn more, discover more and to open to all the potential she had to give and to share.

Blame keeps us entrapped in the past, in something we did or failed to do. We might find ourselves comparing our lives to others whom we think are more successful, attractive, happier, better off, luckier or creative than we are. When we fall short of the mark or ideal we have envisioned, anger, envy, jealousy and a deep sense of sadness may arise. Sometimes the rift between where we are and where we want to be appears too wide to be successfully crossed and we sink into a state of hopelessness or *futility*. Sometimes we need to hit rock bottom and really feel sorry for ourselves and our circumstances before we can make our comeback, before we take hold of our lives, before we take on the responsibility of dedicating ourselves to the spectrum of living rather than the process of dying.

When we allow ourselves to sink into negative moods we feel that we have less worth than others, that we don't deserve anything good, that what we have to contribute has no real value. The Latin word 'futilis' means worthless. Blame, feeling trapped, experiencing an inner sense of futility are all states of mind. They are the result of unnecessarily comparing ourselves to others, harshly judging ourselves, choosing to stay in pain rather than taking the steps necessary for bringing about constructive and positive change. Suffering is an inevitable aspect of life. Often through our suffering the real meaning and purpose of life is discovered. But suffering isn't the way of life; it isn't what life is about. How we deal with our suffering and the attitude we develop toward it is all important.

In his outstanding book, *Man's Search for Meaning*, Viktor Frankel writes of his experiences in a Nazi concentration camp during the second World War:

> "We who lived in concentration camps can remember the men who walked through the huts comforting others, giving away their last piece of bread. They may have been few in number, but they offer sufficient proof that everything can be taken from a man but one thing; the last of the human freedoms—to choose one's attitude in any given set of circumstances, to choose one's own way. And there were always choices to make. Every day, every hour, offered the opportunity to make a decision, a decision which determined whether you would or would not submit to those powers which threatened to rob you of your very self, your inner freedom."

We aren't in a concentration camp, yet we imprison ourselves through negative self-attitudes, guilt, looking on the dark side of life and insisting on seeing what we *lack* rather than all we have to *give*. We have the power and opportunity to do anything we choose to do. To learn to love and be loved is to dedicate our lives to the joy and adventure of living.

The power of love is immense. Harnessing that power and using it to create, to extend our hand to another, to share kind thoughts and encouragement, to be grateful for all that we have and all that we can be, rather than dwelling obsessively on our needs and deficiencies, should be our only goal. We are never healed alone. All healing comes from working together; it comes naturally from recognizing our Oneness with every person we meet and knowing that we are their teacher and they are ours. To love and be loved is an act of courage; for it takes courage to risk, to see ourselves and our lives in a new light, to move ahead despite doubts and fears, to honestly and courageously face ourselves and to do and to say what we know in our hearts is a reflection of our inner truth.

As Viktor Frankel has written:

> " . . . for the first time in my life I saw the truth as it is set into song by so many poets, proclaimed as the final wisdom by so many thinkers. The truth—that love is the ultimate and the highest goal to which man can aspire. Then I grasped the meaning of the greatest secret that human poetry and human thought and belief have to impart: The salvation of man is through love and in love."

SEEKING APPROVAL. We all need attention and a sense of acceptance and accomplishment. But, the burning need to be successful has reached epidemic proportions in our culture. From a very early age we are taught that our success is measured by how much we accomplish in the outer world, the position we hold, the amount of money we make, the car we drive, the property we own, the neighborhood we live in.

All of these so-called accomplishments are wonderful. The problem arises in our personal relationship to them. How important are they to our sense of worth? What do we have to do, how much do we have to accomplish and how much approval do we need from others to feel okay? What do we have to do in order to feel accepted? The fact is, no person, thing, possession or worldly success can ever give us a sense of worth if we don't love, respect and fully accept ourselves. What this means is that nothing outside of us can rescue us from our inner sense of loneliness and despair; nothing outside of us can give us peace of mind.

Seeking approval is often a mask we wear, a role we play, a script we rehearse to *fit in.* Our culture is particularly concerned with doing that which is acceptable, appropriate, with the 'in thing,' to wear, buy, own and achieve. Our statisticians construct charts which teach us about national averages, percentages, classifications and ages so that we can compare ourselves to others as to progress and social status. Instead of seeing the absurdity of such information and research many of us take the data as a sign of our own personal failure, as an indication of being better or worse than the general population, of being okay, or not okay, in the mainstream or off on a tangent. Some look at such graphs and laugh, some get depressed, others respond with apathy and give up, some spend their whole lives struggling to get to the top of the graphs with the 'haves' (as opposed to the 'have nots' at the bottom of the graphs).

How deeply trapped we are in seeking approval depends on how tenaciously we hold onto our illusions of what will make us happy and bring us a feeling of success. We are a culture of consumers. We are always trying to fill ourselves up from the outside. We have learned that *to have more* is better. If that kind of thinking is true, then it follows that to have more is to be more; to have less is to be less. But what do we mean by more and less? Does having more of anything—whether it be cars, money, a Ph.D., hair, or clothing—really say anything about who we are inside?

Having more or having less is a constant struggle, and obsession, in our culture. At one stage of our lives we want to be older and then when we are older we want to be younger. We want a lot of hair *there*, but spend thousands of dollars to remove it someplace else. We want beautiful skin and so we lighten it, darken it, rub lotions on it, massage it, paint it, tighten it and remove it. But what about what's inside? What is underneath the skin, below the surface; how do we feel about ourselves inside? How deeply are we committed to really knowing who *we* are; not who we are expected to be, should be or ought to be?

I remember speaking to a friend who told me that for years she based her acceptance or non-acceptance of herself on the numbers which appeared when she weighed herself on the bathroom scale. If the numbers were high, she disliked herself and her whole day was ruined. If the numbers were low, the day was beautiful. And one day, as she stood on the scale for her 'weigh in,' she suddenly realized that she was judging her life by those three numbers, that three little numbers controlled how she felt about herself. The day she choose to let herself realize this, the day she chose to see that she was a beautiful person despite what the scale said, was the day she began to lose weight. But this time it was for herself, not someone else's image. She soon loved herself even though she was over-weight. But the acceptance had to come from within.

According to Michael Washburn and Michael Stark:

Life is full of examples that demonstrate the futility of the quest for recognition and approval. It is a common occurrence for people to use such expressions as "If only such and such, then I would be happy." A possible life scenario might be: (1) if only I had more friends; (2) if only I were recognized as being a talented athlete, musician, student, etc. (3) if only I had a college degree; (4) if only I could meet the right person; (5) if only I could get a good job; (6) if only I could get a better job (home, car, wife, husband); (7) if only I could make a name for myself; (8) if only my children were successful; and so on right up to the point of death. The assumption in each case is that if this one condition were met, then, identity, worth, and therefore happiness, would be achieved. Yet when one of these conditions is met, rather than experiencing lasting satisfaction, a new condition arises that is seen as the one that will finally do the trick, and so on indefinitely.

The seeking of approval and recognition begins when we are children. We slowly learn that if we act a certain way and say certain things mom and dad feel we are *good*, and if we do things which are irritating they consider us *bad*. When we go to school we learn that the more we conform to what the teacher wants the higher grade we get and the better student we are considered.

When I was an undergraduate major in English Literature I quickly found out that if I interpreted poetry in the same way that the teacher interpreted it, I was given an "A" or a "B." But if I saw a different meaning than the teacher, I was given a "C" or told that I wasn't getting the *real* meaning. I came to realize that the teachers were implicitly telling me: "If you keep seeing the way we see we'll give you an excellent grade. But if you keep on insisting that what you see is valid, you'll never make it to graduate school!" Subsequently, I left that department and majored in Psychology where every idea and theory isn't necessarily true or false. Finally, I found a place where I could be creative, a place where I could think independently.

The media is one of our main teachers in establishing our priorities: If I accomplish or succeed at *that*, people will really take notice. If I smell like *that*, women will be buzzing around me! If I dress like *that*, men will find me sexy! If I wear *that* deodorant, men will be more likely to ask me out! If I rub *that* lotion on my body everyday, my life will be transformed!

The message is this: if we can show the world that we are attractive and desirable and can actually prove it, we will feel happy, fulfilled and accepted. But the fact is, the more determined and obsessed we are with proving our worth, the more uncertain, unsure and fearful we become. This can only lead to inner dissatisfaction and frustration because we are caught up in someone else's image of what we ought to be.

We often get obsessed with the needs of the 'I.' This isn't to say that the 'I' isn't important. The fact is, 'I' am important and the needs and desires 'I' have are important. I have places to go, people to meet, new things to discover, mountains to climb, ideas to share, love to give and receive. The 'I' we often get obsessed with is the "I" that believes that it can never get enough, be enough, have enough, own enough, prove enough, achieve enough to be *okay*. It is the 'I' that is always followed by a 'should.' It is the 'I' that usually feels alone, separate, lost, confused and is so self-absorbed and insecure that life is viewed and lived as a constant struggle. It is the 'I' that is always protecting and defending the role we have chosen and the little image of the self we identify as 'me.' It is the 'I' that is afraid to reach out, to touch another, to risk, to change, to look within.

In *Memories, Dreams, Reflections,* Carl Jung wrote:

> "Only if we know that the thing which truly matters is the infinite can we avoid fixing our attention on futilities and upon all kinds of goals which are not of real importance. Thus we demand that the world grant us recognition for qualities which we regard as personal possessions: our talent or our beauty. The more we lay stress on false possessions and the less sensitivity we have for what is essential, the less satisfying is our life. We feel limited because we have limited aims and the result is envy and jealousy. If we understand and feel that in this life we already have a link with the infinite, desires and attitudes change. In the final analysis we count for something because of the essential we embody, and if we do not embody it that life is wasted. In our relationships to others, the crucial question is whether an element of boundlessness is expressed. . . . The greatest limitation for us is the 'self'; it is manifested in the experience: I am only that!"

As we learn to love and be loved, we begin to see beyond roles and expectations to the essence of who we are. That doesn't mean that we have to stop bathing in Oil of Olay, but it does mean that our sense of self will no longer depend on whether or not we do. It isn't a matter of smelling wonderful and looking wonderful but of being wonderful, of feeling and knowing we *are* wonderful. Loving and being loved is the discovery that we are only just beginning to know ourselves and that the only real limitations are the narrowness of our thoughts and our perceptions. Loving and being loved is awakening the Self with a capital 'S' reflected in the genuine love and respect we begin to feel for ourselves.

One of the questions that is always asked is whether self-love and self-centeredness are the same. Nothing could be further from the truth. Self-love is an opening to the vastness of who we are and what we can be; self-centeredness reflects a narrowness of outlook, a limitation of our goals, priorities and concerns. Self-love is reflected in doing things which we know in our hearts are good for us and for others, in knowing that what we give to ourselves we give to others and that what we give to others we also give to ourselves. If we focus on how little we have and on what we lack, we will feel we have very little to give. As we learn to love we are able to give more because we know we have so much.

Self-love means that we know we have worth—self centeredness means that we are struggling to prove it. Self-love is expressed in caring about others and about how our decisions affect them; self-centeredness means that we only care about how something affects us. Self-love is a growth choice; self-centeredness is a fear choice. So often our decisions reflect the fear of loss, of not having enough, of not doing enough, of not being accepted enough, of wanting to please to avoid the threat of being alone (even though inside we already feel very much alone and separate). We, therefore, choose that which is familiar, predictable, controllable, acceptable and safe.

Self-love is an act of courage, for it requires courage to look within and to let go of all the misperceptions, illusions, distortions, attitudes, beliefs and past experiences which serve as barriers to knowing ourselves and loving ourselves. We are constantly faced with opportunities to grow, to learn, to deepen and enrich our understanding of ourselves and the path we want to take. Our feelings of inadequacy, hopelessness, and incompetence are created by our thoughts and misperceptions. If we constantly identify with what we can't do, we will never fully discover life as it is today.

In his song, "Vienna Waits For You," Billy Joel sings, "If you're so smart tell me why are you still so afraid?" It's an interesting question. The fact is, FEAR is a reaction to anticipated future problems, failures, mistakes, and disasters. FEAR wears many disguises. It is a chameleon which fosters mistrust, blame, guilt, feelings of worthlessness, and exaggerates our sense of entrapment. Fear intensifies our need to defend the choices we make and to protect our fragile self-image.

We learned to be fearful at home when we were children. Fear is a response to feeling unsafe, unloved, uncertain, over-protected. We learned about fear by our past experiences with how our parents dealt with their fears and the ways they helped us with or reinforced our fears. We learned about fear from our formalized religion training. We learn about fear from being a part of the world paranoia, from the things we read about, the events we watch on the news, the shows we watch on television, and the philosophy of success, competitiveness, winning and losing we learn about in school.

Fear stems from not learning to trust ourselves, our wants, feelings, and creative urges. The fact is, fear is energy. We can use it productively by learning how to approach it, or we can blindly let it control us.

Marilyn Ferguson wrote in the Aquarian Conspiracy:

> "There is a fear of the self; an unwillingness to trust our deeper needs. We worry that an impulsive aspect might take over. Suppose we find that we really want is

dangerously different from what we have. And there is a related fear that we will be sucked into a maelstrom of unusual experiences and, worse yet, that we might like them. Or we might become committed to some demanding discipline; if we were to take up meditation, we might start getting up at five in the morning."

Everyone experiences fear. Sometimes the fear paralyzes us and we end up limiting ourselves and our lives over and over again. Sometimes fear cautions us and helps us to think before we impulsively act. Sometimes fear takes the form of procrastination or perfectionism. But no matter where our fear stems from, it often prevents us from taking risks or from trying anything new; it stops us from being spontaneous and from meeting new people.

So often we want to express a more creative part of ourselves or take a new risk and a little voice deep inside says:

"Don't be foolish" or
"Who do you think you are?" or
"You can't do that!" or
"Better play it safe than sorry." or
"You don't have the talent to do that!" or
"You may make a BIG mistake

I remember reading a sign on a friend's desk which said: "IF YOU ARE REAL CAREFUL NOTHING BAD OR GOOD WILL EVER HAPPEN TO YOU!" Maybe we were told to "Always be careful!" when we were children, or "Don't take chances!" or "Don't trust people!" Perhaps we took a few risks and had our hands slapped or experienced some real disappointments and we made the decision to "Play it safe!"

How many times have we wanted to say, "Yes, I want to do that!" but the little voice inside said, "Wait!", "Forget it!", or "It's not important!"

How many times have we said "Yes!" and quickly followed it with "No!" How many times have we wanted to open ourselves to life and instead ended up limiting ourselves more?

How many fears do we have? We fear change. We fear growing old. We fear abandonment. We fear we aren't lovable. We fear losing ourselves in a relationship. We fear being alone. We fear appearing foolish or making a mistake. We fear risking. We fear not being okay. We fear rejection. We fear losing what we have and, therefore, pay a dozen insurance policies to protect everything from loss. We fear someone will take advantage of us. We fear being vulnerable. We fear being humiliated. We fear losing our power. We fear death. We fear God. But one of the most devastating fears is the fear of not fulfilling our potential and of never finding our purpose for being here. Included in this fear is never finding work that is fulfillng and that we are never going to fully realize all that we are capable of in work, in love, and in expressing ourselves creatively.

Gerald Jampolsky may have put it best in his Love Is Letting Go Of Fear:

> "Fear always distorts our perception and confuses us as to what is really going on. Love is the total absence of fear. . . . Although love is always what we really want, we are often afraid of love without consciously knowing it, and we may act both blind and deaf to love's presence. Yet, as we help ourselves and each other let go of fear, we begin to experience a personal transformation."

We all experience fear and its many expressions and manifestations. But, the more we are able to see how fear criples us, blinds us, distorts reality, and creates illusion upon illusion, the sooner and more effectively we will be able to intervene and interrupt our fear response and challenge the power we have given it.

In the teachings of Don Juan, Carlos Castaneda wrote:

> "Fear! A terrible enemy; treacherous and difficult to overcome. It remains concealed at every turn of the way, prowling, waiting. And if the man, terrified in its presence, runs away, his enemy will have put an end to his quest."
>
> "What will happen to the person if he runs away in fear?"
>
> "Nothing will happen to him except that he will never learn. He will never become a man of knowledge."
>
> "And what can he do to overcome fear?"
>
> "The answer is very simple. He must not run away. He must defy his fear, and in spite of it he must take the next step in learning, and the next, and the next. He must be fully afraid, and yet he must not stop!"

The key word in the above passage is defy. When we defy fear we rebel, not in the sense of attack but in the spirit of not giving up; of not submitting to the fear. When we defy fear we accept and admit that fear is present and that we are approaching unknown territory, the unfamiliar, the unpredictable. And we say:

"Yes, I am afraid and it's okay to be afraid. But I am not going to let fear stop me from doing what I want to do. I am not going to give this fear the power over the direction of my life; I am not going to let fear stop me from doing what I know in my heart I must do. I am going to take the next step and the next and the next and the next."

As we begin to transcend our picture of ourselves and to look beyond the fear to the choices, options, and possiblities that lie within us and before us, we are defying our fear. As we begin to look within to discovering the meaning of life, what we have to offer, what we have to give, what we have to share, and all we want to do, we are defying our fears. And when we can begin to see ourselves as creators of hopes, wishes and dreams, we are opening to love's presence. We must never lose sight of our dreams. In our fear we lose all hope and destroy the wonder and the excitement of our dreams. In our fear we narrow our vision and forget about the importance of honoring our spontaneity, our capacity to enjoy life, of stretching our imagination and expanding our world.

In challenging the power we have given to and continue to give to fear, we must take risks, try new things and trust in our ability to make choices that will enhance life.

In letting go of fear we must:

1. Recognize that we are not our old habits, past experiences, negative self-concepts, and beliefs. Rather, these are learned patterns, habits and illusions which shut love out. We have a lot of unlearning to do.

2. Accept that fear and all its accompanying responses are just ways in which we protect and defend the fragile self-image we identify with. As long as we live in fear, we will never discover our inner strengths, abilities, potential, and power to love.

3. Look upon so called 'problems' and 'obstacles' as opportunities to learn more about how we imprison and limit ourselves and, therefore, learn more about what we really want and need.

4. Know that our thoughts create our reality. What we fear most we attract to ourselves again and again.

5. Open ourselves to facing and releasing the fear, guilt, self-doubt, anger and sadness that we often deny. Many

times our greatest fear is looking within. Respect your needs to see a counselor; join a support group like Alanon, group therapy, self awareness groups, personal growth classes, A Course In Miracles. The point is, defying fear requires that we reach out, get out of our own way and do the things which are good for us, for our well-being and for our continued growth and understanding.

6. Recognize that we are afraid because we are not getting what we want from life and not expressing our true self. What do we want at this point in life? How do we want our life to be different?

7. Know that we are sabotaging love and our self-respect by giving fear control of the direction of our lives. We stay in unhealthy relationships because of our fear of the unknown, our fear of making a mistake, our fear of being alone, our fear of examining what we really want, and our fear of intimacy.

8. Know that we avoid being in relationships because of our fear of being vulnerable, our fear of losing our freedom and individuality, fear of being abandoned, and our fear of losing our power.

9. Recognize that fear disappears at the heart level and the more we learn about ourselves, the more we learn about love and loving; for our very essense is love.

10. Accept that it's okay to be afraid. Fear is just another form of energy that we can use to make life difficult and stop us in our tracks, or challenge the power we have given to the fear and go ahead and do what we want and are afraid to do. Never let fear stop you from risking again and again. Be afriad, but do it anyway!

11. Trust in yourself!

Once I thought I knew what trust was
But then the tests began
And I knew the meaning of failure;
Failure to trust again and again.
It requires so much surrender and so much
courage
To trust myself absolutely.

Reshad Feild
There Is Only To Be

CHAPTER IV

TRUST

Trust doesn't come easy to many of us, particularly when our past memories tell us otherwise. We have all had our share of disappointing experiences in childhood wherein our trust was violated; intimate relationships in which our partner lied to us and deceived us in some way; choices and decisions we made which were unavailing. But the fact is, we have no other real choice but to trust ourselves again and again; for when we don't, life becomes laden with fear, loneliness, and stagnation.

Trusting ourselves is one of the most fundamental needs of life, for when we don't we look everwhere else for answers and approval. No matter what difficulties we may be experiencing in life, the answers and wisdom in taking the next step are always within. Our fears distort our perception; our resentments toward ourself and others keep us stuck in the past. Therefore, our ability to trust and to have a deep faith in life diminishes rather than expands as we get older if we take fewer and fewer risks and live 'cautiously.'

It is important that I clarify one very important point,

and that is the kind of trust I am writing of is not blind, indiscriminate trust, but rather a deep faith and knowing which flows from our intuition. Trust comes from our ability to learn from our past rather than getting stuck in it; it develops from our willingness to take risks and to see our competencies rather than focus on our shortcomings.

Trust, then, is a process of growth and maturation which will continue to deepen and expand if we are committed and dedicated to doing the things and developing the attitudes which enhance it. Many of us live with blinders on and seem to encounter the same difficulties again and again. We don't trust because we don't 'see.' If we really knew how wise and courageous we were, life would be filled with wonder, and adventure. If our image of ourselves is that of a 'failure' or a 'weakling' or a 'loser,' then we will probably attract experiences which confirm our beliefs. But, if we see ourselves as a 'risk-taker' or as a 'success' or as a 'gifted person,' then life unfolds in productive and positive ways. I don't want you to get the impression that having a positive attitude always results in getting exactly what we want. The fact is, *a positive attitude doesn't always work, but a negative attitude does!* The keys are commitment, determination, tenacity, and the willingness to risk and risk again. If we play it safe and don't take risks, our self-esteem suffers and our self-trust lessens.

I have found that learning to trust myself more and more is a twelve-step process. Each step symbolizes climbing another rung of the ladder. The higher I climb, the better and more clearly I see myself in relationship to the whole. Each step opens a door to seeing myself in a new and more vibrant light.

Step 1. Cultivate an attitude of gratitude and

appreciation.

Being grateful means that we see ourselves through loving and compassionate eyes, and when we don't, it is because we have forgotten who we really are. Gratitude means that we remember our talents, abilties, strengths, inner gifts, and all the good we have in our life right now. It is an attitude of thanksgiving and appreciation for all the choices we have, the possibilities that lie before us and within us; for all that we can contribute to the world to make it a better place to live. It is the inner peace we experience when we give in the spirit of love and the 'knowing' that to give is an affirmation of 'having.'

Whenever we see ourselves as lacking or deficient in very essential ways, we close the door to prosperity. An attitude of appreciation has the opposite affect; it opens doors to giving and receiving more. When we feel limited, we create limitation. When we begin to see ourselves as rich and full inside with unlimited potential to experience joy and inner peace, then we have taken a very important step to trusting in ourselves and in the abundance rather than in the perceived scarcity of life.

Developing an attitude of gratitude and appreciation means that we begin each day with a short period of meditation and prayer. Meditation is one of the most wonderful ways to begin our day by putting it into a healthy and wholesome perspective. More on this will be explained in subsequent chapters.

Step 2. Dare to dream, stretch, and to move beyond our current life.

Trust develops as we open the channels to the power of our intuition, imagination, and inspiration. As we learn to 'let go' of our self-doubts and develop a receptive and non-judgemental attitude, we will discover that we will take more risks and do more of the things which bring joy into our life. Many of us have closed ourselves off from our dreams, wishes, and fantasies. Many of us are afraid to dream and to allow ourselves to see beyond where we are to what lies beyond. When we haven't first opened the door to appreciation and gratitude, our dreams and wishes can seem unattainable. As we begin to accept that 'we are never stuck,' no matter where we may be in life, doors begin to open. When we begin to see that we always have many options and choices and that the only limitations we have are those we place on our imagination, we begin to stretch and move ahead...to venture into the unknown...to explore the unfamiliar...to dare to dream.

Step 3. Follow through.

If we have a goal/goals, and inspiration to do or to change something, an idea to write or to make something, it is essential that we follow through. An idea or inspiration only remains that if we don't explore it further, if we don't make a commitment to it's unfoldment. Self-trust diminishes to the extent that we don't follow through in pursuing what we want and in going after what we know in our heart is important to our continued growth and development. Self-trust is enhanced when we make our dreams a reality, when we honor our inspirations, when we follow our hunches and respect the intuitive flashes of insight that arise from a deeper wisdom.

Step 4. Learn to live in the present.

Having goals is exciting and gives life a particular focus. But we must never lose sight of the importance of enjoying the process of living each day to its fullest. Living for the completion of a goal is one of the greatest sources of stress.

Stress is the space between where we are and where we want to be. Living in the present means enjoying the little steps of progress along the way, praising ourselves for our commitment and dedication to the task at hand. It is important to always keep the long term goal in the mind's eye but to not get caught in the trap of, "I'll be happy when. . . . " Living in the present means living one day at a time and enjoying the scenery along the way. It means learning the wisdom of beginning each day anew and knowing that I am wiser and more confident today than when I went to bed last night.

Step 5. Know that life is replete with challenges and lessons.

Here we hold the belief that no matter what difficulty we may be experiencing, it is transitory. A difficult day is just twenty-four hours long. The pendulum swings both ways; we are big enough and strong enough to embrace both the problematical and the joyful. No matter what happens we will be okay! There is a deeper and Higher Power which is always guiding us. Our challenges force us to look more deeply inside, to become more resourceful and to reach out. They help us to become wiser and more compassionate with ourselves and others.

Every 'so-called' failure and disappointment really represents a lesson for us to learn. The fact is, everyone experiences difficulties and challenges which test our patience, stamina, determination, sense of self-worth and self-trust. We are continually confronted with new lessons to learn each and every day. Each situation we encounter and person who comes into our life teaches us important lessons and truths. So often we find ourselves referring to the relationship that didn't work or the goal which wasn't achieved as a failure. WE ARE NOT FAILURES because things didn't turn out as we wanted or expected. NEVER IDENTIFY WITH THE WORD FAILURE. Instead, strive to see each situation as an opportunity to learn, to grow, to understand more about what we want and no longer want.

Step 6. Clarify beliefs and values.

Self-trust increases when what we believe to be true is harmonious with what we value. If WE BELIEVE that we are unlovable, undeserving of love, or sentenced to a relationship devoid of love and intimacy and WE VALUE loving and being loved, then our capacity to trust ourself will slowly subside. If WE VALUE success but WE BELEIVE that we aren't capable of accomplishing much, then our self-trust will continue to erode. What we believe to be true about who ,and what we are is crucial to developing self-trust. And when what we value is diametrically different from what we believe to be true, life seems to just pass us by and we end up getting so much less than we want and deserve. If WE VALUE love, it's because we deserve love and we needn't settle for anything less. When we don't, we are working against the natural grain, so to speak. Values are energy and they need to be acknowledged and given expression. If our beliefs contradict that what we value, then we need to take a long serious look at how our belief system is impinging on our happiness, well-being, and self-trust.

If we have difficulty getting in touch with what we value, then I would suggest looking at the qualities we respect and admire in others. Others are a mirror for us. What we love about them, we have inside of us. If we don't know that, it is only becuase we haven't yet acknowledged or discovered that part of us. The same holds true about what we dislike in others.

Therefore, it is important to take the time to explore places in our life where the disparity between values and beliefs exists and to understand how this incongruity creates unhappiness, inner tension, and thwarts self-trust.

Step. 7. Avoid all or nothing thinking.

Life isn't black and white. We aren't always going to live up to our expectations. If we make a mistake, it doesn't mean that we are failures. If we are at a crossroads and seem unable to make a decision, we need not criticize ourselves. It is important to 'let go' of the negative self-talk, such as, "I can't do anything right," or "I'm always in a dilemma," or "I never come through!"

All or nothing thinking means that we see ourself and life in extremes. We are either on one end of the continuum or the other. All or nothing means that if our performance falls short of being perfect, then we are complete failures. All or nothing thinking sets a standard which makes life very stressful, creates a 'no win' situation, unnecessary self-criticism, disappointment, and adversely affects our ability to trust ourselves.

Step 8. Take inventory of all the things we've done or said that we haven't forgiven ourselves for and haven't forgiven others for.

In 'letting go' of all that we are holding against ourselves and others, we are opening the door to trusting in ourselves and life again. All we refuse to release remains like an open sore. The longer we hold onto what happened in the past, the more areas of our life will be negatively affected. How can we possibly trust in a bright future when we are still viewing the past with resentment, blame, and vindictiveness? What purpose does holding on to past hurts and disappointments serve now?

Step 9. Let go of the 'should' statements, 'I can't beliefs, and 'if only I had done . . .' tapes.

These three foster feelings of despair and helplessness. They diminish our efficacy. A 'should' statement is laden with guilt; 'I can't' exaggerates our feelings of entrapment and powerlessness; 'if only' perpetuates our self-doubts, an attitude of lack, and being stuck in the past. Spend some time taking a good look at how many of these self-effacing statements and attitudes we are still holding onto.

Step 10. Cultivate a sense of humor.

This is certainly one of our greatest strengths. Most of us take life much too seriously. We are a culture obsessed with solving problems. If we currently don't have a problem, we either create one or look for someone else's to worry about. So often we forget the simple truth, life is to be enjoyed.

Cultivating the ability to laugh at our melodrama and seeing life in a lighter and more playful way is one of the keys to happiness. When we can laugh at what appeared to be so terribly serious, it is an indication that we are beginning to really see. When the Zen student finally unravels the perplexing koan or riddle, he/she often bursts into laughter. Laughter is an elixir; it is an internal massage. To be in touch with our sense of humor is one of the most joyful and healing experiences of life.

Step 11. Accept and embrace our humanness.

Each one of us experinces a multitude of emotions; disappointment, sadness, joy, fear, anger, resentment, etc. Self-trust unfolds to the extent we unconditionally accept and embrace all of our feelings. The more self-judgments we hold onto, the less self-trust we possess. If we are continually placing conditions on our self-acceptance, we will probably find that we are always raising the ante. In other words, once we get caught up in the cycle of 'having to do such and such BEFORE we will love and accept ourselves,' we will probably never achieve our goal. If our basic underlying belief is, 'I am not enough,' we will never be able to accomplish enough, do enough, or succeed enough to meet our satisfaction. Self-trust begins with the statement, 'I am enough right now!'

Step 12. Make a commitment to live each day with courage, passion, and a deep felt love.

Self-trust develops to the extent we live courageously, and passionately. This means that we engage life and open to life more each and every day. Love is extension. As we begin to follow a path that embodies love, we will discover that love is what we are. When we begin to get into the habit of doing the things we love and want to do, thinking the thoughts which empower us, and making choices which expand our awareness of our unlimited potential, we are on our way to opening the doors to trusting in ourselves and in the bounty of life.

By embracing unconditional love you surrender all emotions and thoughts that separate you from well being and harmony. This is the essential commitment in transformation and it must be renewed every day. Love is a daily celebration of aliveness and permission to go deeper.

Richard Moss
The I That Is We

CHAPTER V

UNCONDITIONAL LOVE

Unconditional love (loving without expectations or conditions) can seem to be an awesome and unattainable goal. As an ideal it seems almost too good to be true. When I tell my class we are going to explore what 'unconditional love' means, a silence falls on the room. I had difficulty with the concept for a long time, myself, until I finally came to see that the problem was in the very question I was asking. It wasn't "how can I love unconditionally?" but rather "how else can I love but unconditionally?"

Unconditional love begins within each of us. It is a reflection of how honestly and openly we relate to ourselves and to others. Loving unconditionally means that we are dedicated to the process of 'letting go' of the obstacles to our happiness and peace of mind. Loving ourself unconditionally means that we see the wisdom of self-acceptance; that we experience the joy and freedom of 'letting go' of the past.

Of course, we want to transcend the elements in our past which inhibit and restrict us from living more spontaneously and fully. But, it is equally important to extract from the past lessons which we might have learned from them. We often cling to painful past events, without realizing there is anything to be learned or understood from them. Our past is our teacher and if it serves us as anything less, then we aren't really allowing ourselves to see it clearly. But we can learn from our so-called 'mistakes' rather than letting ourselves become obsessed with their affect on us. As we begin to open to what unconditional love means, we discover that we always have a choice and our choices free us. We are never really stuck, but rather indecisive, afraid and apathetic. Our attitude is what is conditional.

Unconditional love means that we accept the child within us. Sometimes we act like spoiled brats. Sometimes we whine. Sometimes we are timid. Sometimes we need to be cuddled and held and told that everything is going to be okay. If we can just accept those times and needs, we are on our way to loving ourselves unconditionally. We don't need to place conditions on how we act, the way we speak or the manner in which we behave before we love and accept ourselves. We don't need to act with disgust and criticism for having the needs we sometimes have and for feeling the way we sometimes feel. But we also don't need to feel stuck in our neediness. We have needs, we react, sometimes we regress, sometimes we act like a little child and pout. This is just part of us; not a part to cling to and to get lost in, but simply a part to accept, experience, feel, embrace, and to let go.

We must also accept the curious child in us who gets totally absorbed and lost in exploring the unknown and unfamiliar. Our inquiring mind wants to learn, to understand, to extend and expand the little space we live in. We also need to nurture the inner child who dreams, fantasizes, imagines, day dreams. Can we allow our minds to wander to distant realms, surreal realms, future possibilities and those farther reaches of human nature the late Abraham Maslow wrote so eloquently about? And then there is the inner child who longs to get totally engrossed and lost in a game, a movie or just the moment. When we nurture this inner child and respect its needs, we can play, laugh, sing, dance, and stop worrying about appearing foolish. Isn't it wonderful when we can open ourselves to being as foolish and silly as we want to be and not be concerned with what others are thinking or saying?

There is an inner child we want to free ourselves from, one who feels all alone in the world and who associates love with pain, caring with anger, closeness and acceptance with performance level. To love unconditionally means to open our hearts to this inner child who wants so much to be heard, to share and to love and be loved.

To love unconditionally we must also learn to accept the goal-directed adult in us without losing sight of our need to relax, play and not take life too seriously. It means finding fulfilling work for that adult so that it may feel it is contributing something to the world. The adult in us takes risks, sets goals, plans. This process can be exciting and enriching if we can maintain a balanced perspective in honoring the needs of our inner child.

As children and certainly as adults we've learned the importance of being right. A *Course in Miracles* poses the question "would you rather be right or happy?" This is an excellent question for everyone to ask themselves. Being right is the major criteria by which we most often evaluate ourselves and our lives. There is a spectrum, a lot of space between being right and being wrong. We can compromise, we can explore other options, we can find a middle ground. We don't have to see the world as black or white, successful or unsuccessful, rational or irrational, right or wrong: these are all conditional.

As we open the door to perceiving ourselves and our lives in a new light, we can see the wisdom in not getting stuck in any one concept of who we are or of who others are. Unconditional love embraces the whole person and does not attempt to limit or to judge but rather to accept and transcend.

How rigidly are you living your life and how confining are your attitudes toward your true capabilities?

How many options have you explored and entertained?

How many conditions and misperceptions are you living under?

Spend a little time answering the following questions. They are sentence completion questions and all you need to do is to be honest, truthful, not hold back and let your responses flow.

1. If I didn't have this current job I would _____
_____
_____

2. If I weren't so concerned about what my marriage partner, boy/girl friend thought, I would _____
_____
_____

3. If I didn't live here, I would live in _____
_____

4. If I had more money I would _____

5. If I could live the last 5 years over again I would _____

6. If I were younger I would _____

7. If I forgave myself for everything I'm holding against myself I would _____

8. If I had a happier childhood I would _____

9. If I didn't care about what others would say or think, I would love to _____

10. If I could live out just one of my fantasies, I would

11. If I could travel to anyplace in the world I would go to

12. If I stopped blaming others I would _____

13. If I weren't so afraid of what might happen, I would

14. If I could do anything I wanted to do today and this were an 'ideal' day, this is what I would do from the time I awoke to the time I went to bed _____

_____
_____
_____
_____
_____
_____
_____

_____

15. If I could go back to school, I would study _____

_____

16. If I listed 5 goals I wanted to fulfill in the next 12 months, they would be:
   1.
   2.
   3.
   4.
   5.

17. If I trusted myself more, I would _____

_____

18. If I could love myself more unconditionally, I would

_____

These 'if' statements are not intended to make you think that if the condition were met then you would be happy and fulfilled. Rather, they are intended to help you search and look within to all the *excuses* you use to not move on with your life. An excuse is a condition and a barrier we have constructed that prevents us from reaching any goal over which we feel a conflict. We have job excuses . . . ! "I've done this so long I don't know what else to do" or "this job offers me a lot of security even though I hate it!"

or "others won't like me or approve of my behavior if I do what I want. . . . " And so we may end up doing nothing and resenting others and hating ourselves.

We have early childhood excuses, "if I had a happier childhood I wouldn't be so . . . " We hold onto the tragic and unfavorable conditions of our childhood to avoid taking any responsibility for what we can do now. The next five years doesn't have to be the same as the last five years. What we didn't get, but wanted, when we were three may not be what we need at thirty-five but we are constantly trying to get it any way. If we are always looking back at what was missing when we were four years old we will never discover life as it is today. We can learn a lot about ourselves from our past but we don't have to live there.

How many of us secretly think of going back to school, but are too afraid to actually do it? We make excuses that we are too old, it's too late, it's too competitive, our partner wouldn't approve, there isn't time.

But it is these very attitudes and conditions that are the barrier standing in the way of our opening to our own unlimited potential. When we begin to see unconditional love as the 'yes' that expands, extends and opens us to the realm of the infinite, the possible, to what we can do *now*, the transformation has begun.

Use your answers to these questions as a way of clarifying how you want your life to change, how you want it to be different, what you would really like to do, experience, express and learn more about. The barriers are in our beliefs, our minds, and our attitudes. As we open to the desires and needs of the heart, we are moving on the right path toward the love we need and want to give. Not on the path of what we learned to be true or what we are supposed to do or what seems to be logical or rational, but rather to what we want at the deepest level because it is a reflection of our inner truth.

Sometimes the serious Zen student regards looking beyond our current life situation as a distraction that takes us away from really living in the moment. But the dream is the moment, too. It is a door that, in that moment, we have passed through to a place in our inner depths. These inner places are just as real as outer places and they need to be heard and acknowledged. To love unconditionally is to cherish those precious moments: the one you are living in right now, the one that reflects back to a time when . . . and the one that looks ahead and beyond.

To love unconditionally is to remove judgments and comparisons from our thinking. When we unnecessarily judge ourselves or another we place conditions on both. To love unconditionally is to accept ourselves fully: where we've been, where we are and what we want to attain. As we open to the loving energy within, our behavior will extend that love to ourselves and to others. As we learn to respect our needs and work toward doing the things and nurturing the attitudes which bring us an inner sense of peace, we are laying the foundation upon which we will be able to respond more lovingly and healthily to the needs of others.

When we attempt to offer our love to another from an inner sense of lack, we have already placed barriers or conditions on that love. Sometimes the question we find ourself entertaining is, "Will you still love me if/when . . . ?"

The possibilities are endless in completing this inner dialogue. The following represents just a few examples:

Will you still love me when/if . . .
   I make a mistake?
   You really get to know me?
   I am old?
   I don't have beautiful skin?
   I change?
   I don't get good grades?
   I disappoint you?
   I am bad?
   I do something which you don't like?
   I tell you the truth as to how I really feel?
   I let the little frightened child within me surface?
   I don't live up to your expectations of me?
   I fail at something?
   We disagree and don't see things the same way?
   I need to express myself in ways which threaten you?

This inner dialogue tells us a lot about how inadequate, unsure, insecure and frightened we feel about ourselves. Unconditional love means giving ourselves permission to be human, that we are accepting the full range of emotions and reactions we experience. Sometimes we are threatened, sometimes we feel like we are drowning, sometimes we feel overwhelmed, sometimes we feel lost and confused, sometimes we feel jealous and resentful, sometimes we don't know what we feel, where to turn, or what to do. We must embrace these experiences with compassion, sensitivity and an unconditional regard for our own humanness.

At these times we must try to remind ourselves there isn't anything wrong with us, instead there is something right with us. We might think that what we are feeling is wrong, but the truth is there is something deep within us that needs to be opened to, expressed, and looked at. We aren't going crazy but rather going sane.

Our feelings aren't the problem, rather it is our judgment of ourselves and what others may think that is the problem. If we don't face our own pain, how are we ever going to understand another's? If we don't face our own fears, how will we ever be sensitive to and responsive to another's fears and trepidation?

As we open to and accept our feelings, for whatever they may be at a given time, we have taken an important step to accepting and unconditionally loving ourselves. We may need to work through and live with the feelings for a while, to really let ourselves get depressed, to really allow ourselves to get angry. That's *okay*. At this particular point in time this is what we need to do. It is part of growing, learning, understanding, opening, releasing and letting go. And we must never forget that when we are ready, we can always let go.

Unconditional love is an act of surrender. When we surrender we open ourselves to all of what we are, free ourselves from the messages, beliefs, and attitudes which act as limits or conditions to opening to our higher and deeper needs. Surrender is an act of faith and trust in the gifts we have within us to share and in the Creative Power that is always guiding us and working through us if we will just listen.

Awakening the heart involves a double movement: both letting others into us, which allows us to appreciate their humanness, and going out to meet them more fully. . . . Heart is not only the open, receptive dimension of our being, but also the active, expansive opening out to the world.

John Welwood
Awakening the Heart

CHAPTER VI

AWAKENING THE HEART

Our cultures' values are going through a period of reassessment and reevaluation. It isn't enough to have a career, drive a new car, own a home, have money in the bank, a wrinkle free face, a Visa Gold card, and Calvin Klein underwear. While some of these are certainly satisfying and important, they are never enough in themselves because they don't satisfy the deeper yearnings of the soul.

There is nothing wrong with wanting and working toward having any of these. The problem arises in our obsession with and attachment to their acquisition and for judging ourselves and other as OK or not OK for not living up to our culture's standards of success and approval. We can wear and own all the signs and symbols of success and recognition, but unless we have a deep sense of purpose and meaning in life, a belief that we make a difference and have something of worth to offer and to give, a deeply felt respect and love for ourselves, we will never feel rich and full inside and know what it means to live joyfully. No matter what we want to change about ourselves and our lives, we must always maintain a basic inner regard for who and what we are and for all the positive and beautiful qualities and abilities we already possess. It is this very attitude toward ourselves and our relationship toward life which represents the spirit of unconditional love and loving. At the deepest level of our being we are connected to a Higher Will and Higher Power and if we find ourselves dissatisfied with our lives even though we seem to have everything, we just need to look more deeply within to discover what our true self is saying. Abraham Maslow and Charles Tart referred to this inner disquietude as a search for values; for that which is truly important and meaningful. That which has value adds substance and sustenance to our lives and always brings us closer to our core spritual dimension which is love.

In my studies of Eastern Psychology, I was particularly drawn to the exploration of the centers of consciousness and awareness called Chakras. The activation of these centers of awareness is reflected in the choices we make, what we value, what we give priority to and spend our time and energy doing. In our addictive culture, the two chakras which seem to be most highly developed and expressed are the sensation center and the power center. When our priorities and values are not in balance with the needs of the heart, life always seems to have something missing because the higher and deeper needs aren't being addressed and expressed. If we spend all of our time and energy trying to fill ourselves up with things from the outside, we will never know who we are and what we really want; for we have temporarily lost sight of what is important and essential. As we begin to attune ourselves to a higher and more expansive dimension of experience, our priorities and goals will begin to change and reflect our unique individual needs. This expanded awareness is what transformation is all about.

As we address our higher and deeper needs, we awaken the transformative power of the heart. Richard Moss, M.D., describes it in this way:

> Anatomically the midchest area, is the first metaphorical center of meaning in life and gradually opens into a direct experience of a new dimension. It is the center for the direct sensing of energies that represent unconditional love. It is metaphorical at first because we cannot make unconditional love happen by thinking about it. I tried over and over to tell myself that I could choose love and release a particular pattern, that I didn't need to feel a certain way, and so on. But that didn't change anything. Finally I began to notice where the energy was in and around my body, where sensation was concentrated, and all the thoughts that were part of this state. Then I remembered how I felt when I was in the state of deep well-being and love. Here, as I have said before the energy emanated from the midchest, the heart center. Thus, I finally learned to place my awareness at the heart and began to learn how to transmute energy consciously."

When we begin tapping and expressing our heart energy, it has a transformative effect on the way we gratify our senses and the ways we harness and express our power. We become more aware of the joy of touching another and being affectionate. We want to embrace life and all the beauty which surrounds us. We want to nourish ourselves with good and healthy foods. We become more playful and begin to really listen to what others have to say. When our heart center is awakened, our senses vibrate to all the good things in life and our body becomes a channel for expressing ourselves in new and creative ways.

When our center of personal power is infused with the heart, instead of the ego, we have more energy to work, play, create, and to offer our assistance wherever it is needed. We are no longer obsessed with the need to prove we are right or a successful person, nor do we have a need to control, manipulate, possess, or save another. When our heart center is open, we don't get caught in power struggles of the ego because we recognize that the power comes from a Higher Source.

When we begin to express ourselves more often through the heart, we are relaxed, focused, less reactionary and more responsive to making whatever changes need to be made. When our heart center is awakened we don't try as hard and yet we seem to accomplish more.

The Eastern Psychologies are very consistent in their belief in the necessity of the daily practice of meditation. Meditation is an opening, a bridge, a means to reconnecting with our inner spiritual nature and guidance.

Tarthang Tulku, teacher of Tibetan Buddhism says this of the practice or meditation:

> We may have some idea that a place of ultimate understanding exists; but heaven is not necessarily somewhere else. It is within the nature of our minds, and this we reach through meditation. We just accept each situation as it comes and follow our inner guidance, our intuition, our own hearts.

When the Buddha was asked if he was a king, or a prophet, a God or a saint, he responded that he was none of these. He told his questioners that he was 'awake.' When we are awake, our life looks and feels different to us; for we begin to focus our time and energy on the process of living rather than on simply surviving. When we are awake we take time to notice all the beauty which surrounds us and which lies within us. We are more attentive to nurturing our strengths and abilities and more fully absorbed in the spectrum of life, rather than obsessing on our deficiencies and all we don't have.

Whether you choose to call this 'opening' to ourselves and life more 'aware; or 'awake' makes little difference; for it is the realization that growth comes from trying new things and from taking risks. It is the understanding that we have many options and choices available to us at all times. It is the commitment and dedication to living a more spiritual life. By spiritual, I simply mean that our values, priorities, choices, and goals are increasingly centered in love, gratitude, patience, and inner peace. To love spiritually means that we make fewer and fewer judgements and are more accepting of ourselves and others. It means cultivating the ability to laugh at ourselves and the melodrama we call life. It means living fully in the present while slowly freeing ourselves from the remnants of the past and our obsession with the future. Our spiritual unfoldment and growth parallels deepened and more frequent experiences of joy and in continually seeing the lighter side of life.

Eknath Easwaran describes this transformation in this way:

> As meditation deepens, compulsions, cravings, and fits of emotion begin to lose their poweer to dictate our behavior. We see clearly that choices are possible; we can say yes, or we can say no. It is profoundly liberating. Perhaps we will not always make the best choices at first, but at least we know that there are choices to be made. Then our deftness improves; we begin to live intentionally, to live in freedom.

Years ago, I was given a copy of a beautiful book by Claude Bragdon entitled *Delphic Woman*. In the chapter called 'Passage to India,' the author recounts this Hindu legend:

> In the morning of the world, man, glorying in his power and immortality, so prevailed, through his quality of activity, that he menaced the sovereignty of the gods themselves, and therefore they took away his immortality and afflicted him with death. But when they debated among themselves where they should hide his captured godhead, they were at a loss. For they said: 'Man is a mighty hunter; if we hide it on the highest mountain he will climb it; if we bury it deep in the earth there will he will dig; or if we sink it in the sea he will explore its bottom; there is no place in which he will not seek. But Brahma said: "Give it to me and I will hide it where he will never think to look for it." They aksed him where this might be and he would not tell them, but he hid man's divinity within man himself, and it is indeed there he does not think to seek, but goes unresting up and down the world looking for his lost godhead, overcome by death again and again.

The search for love is our search for our divinity. It is the search for all the divine and Godly within each of us; our compassion, joy, inspiration, creativeness, and peace of mind. In this quest, meditation can tap these inner resources. As we meditate, we slowly let go of the power we have given and continue to give to feeling guilty, fearful, and resentful. A commitment to meditation is a commitment to nurturing and caring for ourselves. It is a dedication to the process of opening to qualities and actions which add perspective and depth to our lives. It is a pathway to restoring balance to our distorted perceptions and to opening to our spiritual eye. This means that we begin to see more clearly because we have opened the channels to the healing power of our intuition.

Psychologist Francis Vaughn says of this experience:

"The willingness to follow the guidance of this inner teacher is trusting intuition. Behind fear, anger, depression, and anxiety is hidden the capacity for love, joy, serenity, and compassion. Behind all emotions is the wisdom of intuition that can lead one to the full experience of the central core of being. The more you are willing to open yourself to the full awareness that is potentially yours, the more authentically you can live your life."

Our minds are constantly evaluating, judging, comparing, analyzing, rationalizing, intellectualizing, and conceptualizing. Mediation helps us to see beyond the endless activity of the mind to the still point where our true creative power lies.

T.S. Eliot wrote:

> At the still point of the turning world. Neither flesh nor
> fleshless;
> Neither from nor towards; at the still point, there the
> dance is,
> But neither arrest nor movement. And do not call it fixity,
> Where past and future are gathered. Neither movement
> from nor towards,
> Neither ascent nor decline. Except for the point, the still
> point,
> There would be no dance, and there is only the dance.

When we meditate regularly, we begin to more clearly see the old habits and responses which get us into trouble. When we meditate we begin to change our relationship to ourselves; we are kinder, more considerate, and more sensitive to what brings us feelings of peace. As we mediate and trust our intuition more, we will find that we are taking more risks, trying new things, seeing possibilities where we once saw a dead end, and see problems as opportunities to learn more about ourselves and all we are capable of.

As we begin this inner journey a whole new world opens up before us because a whole new world is opening within us. We begin to discover new sources of inner strength and power we never realized we had. The emotions which use to cripple us no longer have the impact they once had. We still get angry, have doubts, fears, and feel awkward at times, but in our heart we know we are getting stronger and expressing ourselves honestly, openly, and freely.

I want to share some important guidelines with you on how to most successfully and effectively begin the practice of meditation. I recommend meditating first thing in the morning so that your meditation sets the tone for the rest of your day. In this way you will begin each and every day with positive and uplifting thoughts and attitudes.

1. Find a quiet and peaceful place where you can be alone for 10 to 15 minutes without interruption.

2. Find a straight-back chair or cushion to sit on. Most people find it more comfortable to place the cushion on a carpet and sit with legs crossed. If you sit forward on the cushion, you will find it most comfortable. You can also sit with your back resting against a wall. The important thing to remember is to keep your back straight and to be comfortable.

3. Take 5 minutes to read an inspirational passage from one of your favorite books. The source makes no difference: A Course In Miracles, The Unity Daily Word, Spiritual Meditations of Paramahansa Yogananda, the writings of Eva Bell Werber, The Bible, The Prayer of St. Francis; the choices are limitless. The main thing to keep in mind is that the material needs to be spiritually uplifting and inwardly calming. From this reading you may extract the word/ words which will serve as your lesson for the day, both as

your meditation material and the thought/lesson you will incorporate into all your activities.

When we meditate on a lesson in this way, it is called an affirmation. An affirmation is simply a positive statement of what we want, who we are, what we want to express, what we want to attract, an assertion of what is inherently true. The following are affirmations you may consider reading each morning for a period of 9 days:

Day 1 (Keyword: Peace) I am filled with the Spirit of Peace today. I am calm, relaxed, and serene. Peace is what I want and peace is what I am giving to myself and others.

Day 2 (Keyword: Love) Love surrounds me, enfolds me, protects me, guides me, flows through me touching everyone I meet today. Love is my very essence. To love and be loved is my single goal today.

Day 3. (Keyword: Light) The Light of God is guiding me today in seeing myself and others in a new and positive way. I feel a lightness in my step, a clarity in my thinking, a self-assuredness in everything I do.

Day 4 (Keyword: Prosperity) Prosperity is an attitude. I am very rich and full inside and am free to be all I have been created to be. I am discovering new talents, new interests, and many new ways of attracting more and more prosperity in my life. Prosperity in relationships, prosperity in my work prosperity in my finances, prosperity in my friendships.

Day 5 (Keyword: Abundance) I open the door to abundance: abundance of love and loving, abundance of opportunities, abundance of joy, inner peace, and health.

Day 6 (Keyword: Freedom) I am free; free to make decisions, free to by myself, free to play, free to express my deepest needs, free to enjoy this beautiful day, free to smile, free to laugh, free to change my mind, free to love and be loved. My freedom is one of my most precious gifts.

Day 7 (Keyword: Giving) All that I give to others I give to myself. Therefore I am very aware of what I am giving today, what I am saying, what I am sharing. Giving in the spirit of love is the greatest gift I can share.

Day 8 (Keyword: Potential) I have unlimited potential to love, create, learn, grow, give, and to be happy. Today, I open the door to my vast potential and I let my heart light shine touching everyone I meet.

Day 9 (Keyword: Beginnings) I have renewed faith and trust in myself. I respect myself and accept who and what I am. The past is gone. Today is a new day, a new beginning; I am enthusiastically taking the next step toward the unfoldment of my dreams.

4. Close your eyes. Take a few deep breaths to help you relax and then focus on the words you have chosen for your meditation. This is often the most difficult part. Try to visualize each letter and word. If, for example, your affirmation is: TODAY I OPEN THE DOOR TO MY VAST POTENTIAL TO LOVE, CREATE, LEARN, GROW, GIVE, AND TO BE HAPPY... visualize each word in the mind's eye, one at a time... TODAY... I... OPEN... THE... DOOR... TO... MY... VAST... POTENTIAL... TO LOVE... CREATE... LEARN... GROW... GIVE... AND... TO BE... HAPPY... Repeat these words over and over again. You can say them aloud, gently whisper them, or silently repeat

them. Your mind will probably want to resist the process and the inner mind chatter will begin. Don't get discouraged or annoyed! Don't fight the inner chatter, just let it happen and return to the affirmation and allow each word to penetrate deeply.

5. End your meditation with a prayer. In the highest and most beautiful sense, all meditation is a prayer; a prayer affirming that God is giving you the strength, courage, and the determination to continue meditating and incorporate the lesson into your day. It is a time of prayer when our positive thoughts are sent to those near and dear to us, that their lives be more joyful, peaceful, and loving. Prayer consciously affirms our connectedness to the power of the Spirit within. Prayer affirms that we are not alone but rather held lovingly in the grace of God. Prayer is the medium through which we can express our gratitude and thanks-giving, thereby affirming all that we have rather than seeing ourselves as lacking or deficient. Meditation, then, is a time to give thanks for the opportunity and the challenge of this day we have before us as we deepen our commitment to nurturing attitudes which promote inner peace and harmony.

6. Write your lesson down on a piece of paper and make sure to take it with you wherever you go during the day. You will be amazed at how effective referring to the lesson is. On occasion I have meditated in the park, in the car, in the library, or any other quiet spot I could conveniently use. Many of us have developed the habit of drinking coffee for a mid-day lift. As a suggestion to you, try a mid-day meditation. It is a wonderful source of relaxation, peace, and energy.

If something causes you to become upset, refer to your

lesson for the day. It will help you to refocus on the peace you want to experience. The more you focus and meditate on positive and healthy mental attitudes, the easier it will be to translate them into positive activity. You will find, as I have, that referring to your lesson during the course of the day will be incredibly helpful in reinforcing the affirmation you began the day with.

You may find it relaxing to imagine you are somewhere else as you meditate; walking in a meadow or along the ocean, sitting under a tree, soaring through the sky like a bird. If this helps to promote a more relaxed meditation, then by all means do it. Music is also a wonderful aid to meditation. There are hundreds of new age tapes which will help to promote inner peace and a deep-felt joy.

The following affirmations open up the visual channels. I have found them to be most effective as I both focus on the words and the inner picture of 'doors opening.'

I open the door to love.
I open thd door to self-respect, kindness, and compassion.
I open the door to vibrant health and inner peace.
I open the door to abundance in all its manifestations.
I open the door to joy.
I open the door to discovering my unique path.
I open the door to setting goals and to organizing a plan to accomplish them.
I open the door to learning from and growing from life's challenges and experiences.
I open the door to new friends.
I open the door to my creativeness.
I open the door to giving and to others giving to me.
I open the door to speaking up for what I believe in.
I open the door to making healthy choices.

I open the door to trusting myself more and more.
I open the door to being more playful.
I open the door to laughter.
I open the door to my spiritual development.
I open the door to being happy.
I open the door to self-discovery.
I open the door to my dreams.
I open the door to my inner gifts.
I open my heart to loving and being loved . . .

Sit in a comfortable position, back straight, eyes gently closed, and begin to breathe deeply. This time I want you to count your breath, which will help you improve your concentration.

Inhale for a count of 4, hold the breath for a count of 4, exhale for a count of 4, pause for a count of 4. Repeat this exercise slowly 6 or 8 times and make an attempt to really concentrate on the breathing. Imagine that you can actually see the breath as you draw it in and expel it.

Now bring your attention to your heart center at the mid-chest level. Imagine that you are breathing through this point. If you are having difficulty feeling this center, rub it and the warmth and stimulation will direct your attention there. As you inhale, slowly repeat the words, "I AM FILLED WITH LOVE." As you exhale, repeat the words, "AND I EXTEND MY LOVE." Slowly repeat this process 6-8 times.

Now with your attention on the heart center, meditate on the following words:

Today I am creating the kind of day I want to have. Today is a beautiful day because I am beginning this day with love, filling this day with love, ending this day with love. I deserve love and all the good things life has to offer. Love is mine to give and I willingly and joyfully give it to myself and extend it to others. This is the path to peace.

Now with your attention on the throat center, meditate on the following words:

Today I speak words of kindness, words of encouragement, words which promote harmony, peace, and understanding. Today I choose to be gentler and more constructive with my words. My words reflect how I feel about myself. Today I am confident and self-assured.

Now focus your attention on the center point of your forehead. This is called the point of intuition and center of illumination; the so called, 'third eye.' Meditate on the following words:

Today I am sending positive thoughts and messages into the world. I am blessed with the gift of positive thinking. I have unlimited potential to love and be loved. I have unlimited potential to experience joy and inner peace. My thoughts create my reality and they create the experiences I will have today. I choose gentle thoughts of peace. I choose inspiring thoughts of encouragement. Today I choose healing thoughts of love.

Bring your attention back to your heart center and visualize the light radiating and extending from the heart to the throat to the forehead. Visualize these 3 points vibrating and pulsating with energy. Now begin your focused breathing again, as you inhale and exhale through the heart center. Open your eyes when you are ready.

This meditation can become part of your regular morning meditation or it can be used on weekends when you have more time. It will help you become familiar with your ability to focus on and direct energy to different areas of your body. Thought is energy. If we can begin to change the quality and form of our thoughts, we are on the path to using our energy more creatively and, therefore, lovingly. As we awaken the heart, we open to the loving energy within. The keys to successful and fulfilling meditation are:

1. CONSISTENCY. I couldn't stress this enough. Meditation requires a commitment to making it an integral part of our daily activities. The early stages may require much effort and persistence, but a day will come when our meditation seems effortless.

This process can be compared to the grace of a dancer. When we see the ballerina move softly and lilting across the stage, we forget the incredible amount of work and effort involved in achieving that kind of perfection. Once it is achieved, though, she doesn't stop practicing. But there are days when her dancing ability seems to be waning until she again reaffirms her commitment to the process. Meditation is like that. It requires our time, our perseverance, and our love. If we have chosen to meditate for 10 minutes every morning then we need to follow through and meditate for 10 minutes every morning. It makes no difference whether we are traveling or visiting at a friend's house, we can always find a quiet space to meditate.

2. PUTTING IT INTO PRACTICE. It is important to know that our affirmations and lessons are not just words we repeat and contemplate. They are positive mental attitudes which will translate into positive and enriching activity and behavior. If, for example, you are meditating on experiencing joy and inner peace, it is imperative to the whole process to incorporate activities into the day which are conducive to bringing about feelings of peace and joy.

3. DO NOT JUDGE OR COMPARE. Meditation is often started and tried for a while, then dropped because our expectations aren't instantly met. If we encounter a problem

in meditating or find we are not making the progress we had hoped for, the solution lies in not judging what we are doing or not doing and in having patience with the process. Don't give up and stop, but go deeper instead! Going deeper may require a concerted effort to concentrate more on the lesson, joining a meditation class, attending a weekend meditation retreat, or reading more on the subject of meditation. Breaking through our inner resistance to meditation and to accepting the lesson as truth requires the commitment to stay with it despite doubts, frustration, or fear. It is a commitment we renew each and every morning. In the deepest and highest sense, it is a commitment to nurturing and loving ourselves more each and every day.

I hope that two people can grow together, side by side, and bring joy to each other, without one having to be crushed so that the other may stay strong. Perhaps maturing is also to let others be. To allow myself to be what I am.

Liv Ullmann
Changing

CHAPTER VII

MAKING LOVE THE MOST WONDERFUL EXPERIENCE IN LIFE

Love stirs us on every level and our whole being is transformed by its power and magic. What else can knock us off our feet and sweep us away, excite our senses, arouse our fears, cause anxiety attacks, lighten our step, crush our ego, open our heart, fill our life with joy, adventure, passion, laughter, and buckets of tears (sometimes all in the same day). In the name of love we suffer disappointments and setbacks, experience 'highs' like we've never thought possible, and 'lows' that make us conclude that we haven't learned a thing.

We want so much to love and be loved, yet we are often afraid of being too vulnerable, risking rejection, and allowing another into our inner world. In respnose to past hurts and disappointments, many of us deny ourselves the love and intimacy we so deeply want;   deny ourselves the joy of opening our heart to another.

So often in the beginning stages of a relationship we spend so much time trying to impress each other and hide our perceived weaknesses, that we panic at the thought of being unable to maintain the role.

"How about if he/she finds out how insecure I am and how **many** fears I have? How about if this person really gets to know me and wants to learn more about me? What am I going to do if I begin to really like this person and we begin to fall in love? And what if he/she decides that I'm not likeable and I'm left for someone else? Can I handle the rejection? Do I really want to get involved in the first place? And if so, how involved do I want to become?"

We certainly do worry a lot. Our minds are constantly thinking, probing, questioning. When we begin to take a good look at how many doubts and concerns we have about love and intimacy, it is no wonder that love is viewed as being very complex.

The truth is, we need to lighten our whole attitude and approach to loving and being loved. Why make something which is wonderful so difficult? Why make love into a problem when all love asks of us is that we be ourself and share the beautiful person that we are.

We read and hear so much about the importance of open communication in a relationship, but we must keep in mind that communication is multi-dimensional. First of all, we have needs which must be respected. We have a need to be heard and to know that another is interested in what we have to say. We have thoughts and ideas to share; beliefs and convictions which reflect how we see life, what's important to us and what we value. These experiences are an integral part of healthy and open communication.

When we meet another who shares our sense of life, who has similar interests, values and fundamental beliefs, we experience an intimacy and closeness with another who understands as we understand. And as we open our heart, we become increasingly aware of the importance of listening. Listening is one of the greatest gifts we have to share; for when we listen, without judgement or the need to be right, we are giving another the most precious gift we have . . . ourself.

> "One of my biggest fears of intimacy is losing myself in the relationship. I remember when I met Tom. His energy, enthusiasm and ambition really drew me into his world. I found myself doing what he wanted to do most of the time and didn't really pay attention to what I wanted. When I began to become more independent, he resented it. I tried to talk to him about the difficulties I was experiencing and the needs I had, but he wouldn't listen to me and didn't want to talk about it. As time passed, we became more and more distant. Since I couldn't express what was troubling me, other areas of our life were shut down. Once the communication stopped, the relationship was in real trouble.

> "I've certainly learned a lot about love and what I want from a relationship over these past years. I want to be with someone who is willing to work with me at resolving whatever difficulties arise. I want to complement another's life and I want them to do the same with me. I want to really get to know the person as a friend first and then let things develop slowly and naturally."

Healthy communication requires that we freely express ourselves emotionally. Sometimes we are sad, sometimes we are excited and overflowing with joy, enthusiasm and inspiration; and sometimes we are afraid and overwhelmed with the stresses and challenges of life. True intimacy means that we embrace and accept all that we feel and not pretend that all is well when it isn't. Many of us did not learn that feelings are an integral part of who we are. It is a gift to cry, to laugh, to be angry, to be sad, happy and to feel the passion and creative powers surging through us like a shooting star. The greatest pain comes from our alienation from our own humanness; from hiding and denying the emotions which make us the person that we are.

How can we possibly maintain an intimate relationship with another if we have not been nurturing an intimate relationship with ourself? If we don't allow ourselves the freedom and the room to feel all that we feel, how are we ever going to let another really get to know us? Are we always going to have hidden parts? We often refer to love as a problem, but the fact is, the problem lies in the judgements we make about how we 'should' feel. The problem lies in our expectation that we must always be perfect and that there is something wrong with us for feeling the way we sometimes feel. When we can allow ourselves the freedom to feel and to honestly express all that we are, then we come to discover the power of 'letting go'; of not getting stuck in our feelings.

Emotional communication allows us to enter into another's innerworld and to see as they see, to feel as they feel, to experience life as they experience life. When our feelings are acknowledged and respected, we feel more visible, more accepted for who and what we are, and more deeply loved. And when we open the door to true compassion, we gently allow ourselves the opportunity to become more sensitively and acutely aware of our humanness and our oneness; the realization that each of us wants the same thing . . . to love and be loved.

> "Intimacy means that you really enjoy being with each other, enjoy sharing and doing things together. When two people are in the beginning stages of a loving relationship, the enjoyment of each others' company is usually continually enhanced. This is why I believe that if the relationship is going to last, the two of you must nurture a deep and intimate friendship. If you aren't friends, then

what's the point? The fact is, when you are friends you can disagree, argue, be afraid, and see things differently without adversely affecting the relationship.

Years ago, when I was involved with another man, I knew that the relationship was in trouble because our arguments and disappointments resulted in our feeling more separate. Both of us held onto our accumulated resentments. Instead of us learning from our differences and simply seeing that we were in fact two uniquely different people who could compromise, we tried to change each other and the gulf between us grew wider and wider. Our conflicts superseded the integrity and the common purpose of the relationship. It was painful watching us grow more distant, turning into strangers and enemies instead of growing as friends and lovers.

Growing in love requires honesty. As a matter of fact, I would venture to say that honesty and trust are the two most important qualities in establishing and maintaining a meaningful relationship. Honesty, trust, and communication go hand in hand. If two aren't communicating what they want, what they need, what they are going through, and what they are feeling, then the relationship is dishonest."

Healthy and fulfilling communication has sexual and physical needs which we want expressed. We want to be held, touched, and affectionately caressed; to lie naked with another and feel that wonderul sense of oneness. Sometimes we confuse sex with intimacy and forget that it is an expression of intimacy and is deeply affected by our other modes of communication. Almost every person I interviewed in regard to their views of healthy and fulfilling love making responded that it was directly related to the quality of sharing, emotional openness, genuineness, respect, thoughtfulness, and affection of the two persons involved. In other words, the depth of fulfillment sexually was proportional to the quality of love and intimacy expressed. Their sexual lives were great because of the authenticity in other areas of their lives. They were good friends (something we often forget to be to one another), they respected each other and were openly affectionate.

A relationship that develops and evolves over time which is continually strengthened by these three levels of communication and intimacy takes us to new heights and depths of awareness and understanding. This deepened respect and appreciation for one another is the spiritual dimension of love. The spiritual is the transcendent and luminous power of the relationship which lights our way with faith, commitment, and a desire to help and assist each other in any way we can. The spiritual dimension is reflected in the values we embrace and which guide our lives. As we grow spiritually, the feelings and concerns that use to devastate us, no longer have the power they once had.

As we continue to open the doors to our spiritual Self, we feel more deeply connected to a Power greater than ourself and know that we are part of something that can get us through any crisis if we are willing to 'let go' of the struggle and ask for guidance, clarity, and understanding.

The key to our spiritual progress is the sincerity of our intent; that we are sincere in wanting to make peace of mind our single goal. This doesn't mean that we've achieved sainthood. It does mean that we are wise to the things we do and say which separate us; that we are wiser to the things we do and say which bring us together.

Why, then, are we often afraid of love? What is preventing us from experiencing the kind of love we know in our heart that we want? As we open ourselves to all that we are and begin to unconditionally accept ourselves by 'letting go' of our critical self-attitudes, trusting ourselves more and by being gentler and more compassionate with ourself and others, our life will be fulfilled. This 'lightened' approach to life reflects the true meaning of the word 'enlightenment'; to see ourself and life in a positive and more playful light.

If we only come to know, embrace, and accept a part of who we are, then this is only how much we will let others know, how much we will let others see. All we hide only serves to diminish the power of love and intimacy we so deeply want to experience. To love is the greatest joy of life. To withhold love is the greatest pain.

What you believe you are determines your gifts.

A Course in Miracles

CHAPTER VIII

WRITE A NEW SCRIPT

Writing down the feelings, the guilt, rage, jealousy, blame and fears that are crippling us, is very important and can produce illuminating insights. I would suggest keeping a journal. It is a tool that can help us to become more focused and gain perspective on ourselves and the attitudes which are preventing us from living a more fulfilling and rewarding life.

Let's take an example from an earlier chapter. One of the negative beliefs a young woman had carried around with her for 30 years was, "Love is a disappointment to me. I just don't trust!" Write this message on a piece of paper and add the word "because" at the end. Now repeat the sentence over and over to yourself until you begin to feel an emotional connection to it and what you are saying.

Here is how the process can work:

"Love is always a disappointment to me and I don't trust because . . . I always get hurt. . . . because I've gotten hurt in the past. . . . Love is a disappointment to me and I don't trust because . . . love was never there for me when I was young . . . I waited and waited. . . . Love is a disappointment to me and I don't trust because . . . I expect to get hurt . . . because I don't believe that I am ever going to be happy. . . . Love is always a disappointment to me because . . . I guess I just don't like myself. . . . I am a disappointment to me . . . how have I disappointed myself?

"Why don't I trust myself? . . . because . . . here I am in my 30s and still stuck in the past. . . . I am disappointed about love and believe I'll get hurt because I've gotten hurt before. . . . I expect to get hurt . . . I believe I will get hurt . . . I focus on it . . . because . . . I know what it's like to not really have a loving relationship . . . to fear relationships . . . to always anticipate the worst . . . to always settle for so little . . . love is a disappointment to me because . . . I believe it is . . . And what is the alternative? being alone, protecting myself, anticipating the worst will happen . . . needlessly suffering and worrying. . . . Love is a disappointment to me because . . . I don't trust that I really have much to offer another . . . I really don't have much to give and to share . . . I'm afraid to get that close, to be that vulnerable . . . I want so much to express my love . . . I want so much to like myself . . . I want so much to know myself. . . . Love is a disappointment to me and I don't trust because . . . I am living in the past . . . I seem to be stuck in the past . . . (and end with this thought) because . . . I am choosing to feel this way right now."

Accepting the responsibility for our thoughts and attitudes and knowing that the choices we make create our reality is essential to changing them. If we realize that we are not victims and that the experiences of the past are dictating our current disappointments, then we are on our way to seeing that we can, indeed, do something about it . . . but only if we choose to.

Knowing that we have a choice and that we can unlearn and reverse our old toxic inner messages is a very powerful insight. It may not seem like we have a choice, but we do. We can choose which voice we are going to listen to, which messages we are going to pay attention to, which words we are going to believe.

If we are going to begin to reverse old patterns and beliefs we need to use our time and energy in expressing what we really want and what we really are, rather than continuing to give power to our old illusions and misperceptions of who we are and what we *should* want.

Let's take the above scenario as an example. The writer's experience was that 'love was disappointing.' She just didn't trust that love could turn out any other way. One of the key things she said, was that she didn't like herself, didn't know herself, and didn't have much to offer or to give.

Next, let's take one of the affirmations we listed earlier, in the chapter on meditation and look at the two beliefs set side by side. An affirmation is a positive statement about who we are, what we want, what we want to express, and what we want to attract to ourselves. An affirmation is an inner truth.

What I believe to be true: I don't like myself, I don't know myself, I have little to give.

What is true: I am very rich and full inside and am free to be all I have been created to be.

If we choose to live by what our past experiences tell us is true, we know what to expect. Even if life is unfulfilling and uneventful, it is manageable, predictable and, in an unhealthy way, understandable. We can say, "love is a disappointing experience. It was disappointing when I was a child and all my love experiences since then have been the same." We have a built-in excuse as to why love eludes us.

We can feel sorry for ourselves. We can avoid taking any responsibility for what we are doing to perpetuate this old pattern. We can blame and complain . . . if we choose to. We can seek relief from our pain and frustration in drinking, eating, drug use, television, get lost in a romance novel . . . if we choose to. OR we can choose to look and see the truth within, taking yet another step on the path to turning life around.

Looking within seems to be the most frightening step of all; but as the old adage goes, only the truth will set us free. The following exercise can help you look within . . . if you choose to.

1. *Write down the above affirmation.* After you have written it, write the word 'but' and complete your thought. Chances are you will not believe in the power or truth of the affirmation yet. The process might go something like this: "I am very rich and full inside and am free to be all I have been created to be. But I don't feel free. I feel stuck and

I really don't know about my so-called potential and gifts. Right now it takes enough of my time and energy just to get by."

2. Write the affirmation and follow it with your thoughts once more. "I am very rich and full inside and am free to be all I have been created to be ... but I feel so entrapped, I'm afraid. I have so many fears and concerns. I want so much to love myself and to share my life with others, to discover what I am capable of doing and being. But I just feel so lost right now."

3. Write the affirmation again 3 times, but this time add: "If I felt totally free I would _____

4. Close your eyes and momentarily allow yourself the freedom to do anything that you want to do, to be any place you want to be, with anyone you wish to be with, working at any job you'd really like to have. Imagine what you'd like to accomplish for yourself, for others, for the world. You have many gifts to offer, so much potential to express.

5. Share your dreams and visions with your journal.

6. Share this experience with one other person: a close friend, your counselor or just someone you trust very much. The experience of sharing our heart's deepest desires has a liberating effect.

7. Meditate on this affirmation. The meditation will help you to concentrate on that which affirms our inner truth. The more we allow ourselves to open to attitudes and thoughts which extend and expand our awareness, the more we are being loving with ourselves.

8. Know that we attract what we believe to be true about ourselves. If we are determined to believe that disappointing love experiences are what we really deserve from life, then we will just have to accept all that goes with it, namely, a life full of suffering, disappointment and pain.

9. Cultivate the habit of writing. As you write down all your negative inner thoughts and beliefs, remember it is important to the process that you end with two thoughts: 1) I don't know myself. 2) I am choosing to feel this way and see myself this way. Our feelings of unworthiness, guilt, fear, separateness, all the blaming we do, all the suffering, stems from *not knowing ourselves*. The more time we spend affirming the positive things that are inherently ours to experience and to examine, the more we look within and commit ourselves to express our healthiness, the more satisfying and enriching our life will be.

10. You might find it helpful to date the material you write. That way you can look back and see what you were experiencing at a particular point in time. This can add breadth and perspective to your inner work.

11. Nurture a sense of humor. Life may not seem to particularly humorous at this time. Most of us live our lives as 'reruns.' How many times can you watch the same movie before you walk out and move on? How many times do you have to experience the same *drama* before you have had enough? But if we can learn to laugh at the *inner soap opera* we seem to live through again and again, we have taken a very essential step toward healing, health, and growth.

12. Remember, life becomes an emotional see-saw whenever our integrity is in question. Our stomachs are

emotional barometers for how happy, peaceful and loving we are feeling. When we are not being honest with ourselves and expressing what we know in our hearts we want and need, we find ourselves in pain. We always know inside when something essential to our integrity is missing from our life. We know when our lives have gone awry. Use your journal at these times, choose one affirmation that seems the most appropriate at the moment and work with it.

13. Use the journal to share all the good feelings and good things which are happening in your life. Don't spend all your time writing down negative maudlin thoughts and feelings. Share your insights, list the goals you want to achieve. If you discover a new interest, make a new friend or just had a lot of good things happen today, write them down. Relish them. Enjoy them. Appreciate them and appreciate yourself for opening to the good experiences of life.

14. Ask yourself pointed questions, carry on a dialogue with yourself in the journal. Ask yourself why you do things that aren't fulfilling, what you fear most, how you are stuck at this particular junction in your life, what you don't want in your life anymore, what aren't you giving to yourself? Share these answers and insights with another person.

15. Use your journal to develop a plan to bring about the changes you want in your life. Every problem has an answer. Sometimes we are afraid to allow ourselves to even mentally explore the areas of our lives we want to improve. When what we want is dramatically different from what we have, our goals will disrupt our current life script. Are we willing to give that up? What are we willing to do to express ourselves in new ways? How much are we willing to risk?

What do we stand to lose? These are important questions to ask ourselves and explore as we write.

16. Write unsent letters. This can be a very powerful exercise. If there is someone you have a lot of feeling about, and a lot of unfinished business with, write them a letter. Sometimes we are unable to muster the courage to speak to someone directly or feel so angry or hurt that we are unable to effectively say what we really want to say in person, writing them an unsent letter can be a very healing experience. After you have written the letter you can decide if you really want to send it or not. It is very helpful to write this letter, even if the person we wish to address has passed away. It can still help us clarify and release many of the feelings, concerns and attitudes about them which have been suppressed.

17. Write your affirmation/positive statements and carry them with you and refer to them many times during the day. This is a most effective way of reinforcing the positive thoughts you want to incorporate into your life. Remember! Only the affirmation is true. If you continue to listen to the old tape and continue to believe that it is true, you are caught in a struggle of wills between your critical/judgmental self and your Higher Self. The old tapes are difficult to 'let go,' so don't berate yourself for your periods of depression, times of feeling sorry for yourself, and the like. We all go through these periods, but it doesn't mean we have to get stuck there. To break the old patterns requires we be gentler with ourselves and have compassion for our own humanness.

Finishing business means that I open my heart to you, whatever blocks my heart with resentment or fear, that whatever I still want from you, is let go of and I just send love. I let go of what obstructs our deepest sharing. That I open to you as you are in love. Not as I wish you to be or as I wish me to be. An opening into the oneness beyond the need to settle accounts. No longer looking to be forgiven or to show others how unfair they were. To finish our business, we must begin to stop holding back. Gradually love replaces clinging. As we begin to open past our image of some separate "me" in relationship to some separate "other" and just be there with ourselves in soft openness, our business is finished.

Stephen Levine
Who Dies?

CHAPTER IX

LOVE IS FORGIVING

Forgiveness isn't easy. As a matter of fact, it is very difficult. We can't seem to forgive others for what we feel they've done to us because we haven't yet forgiven ourselves for what we believe we've done. The same principle applies to expressing love; we need to open the channels to loving ourselves first, before we are really ready or able to love another. When we don't respect and love ourselves, we search everywhere for someone, or something to heal the inner rift. Forgiveness is one of the most important pathways to this healing.

To begin forgiving ourselves, we need to ask a few very important questions.

1. *What are all the things we've done and said that we have not forgiven ourselves for?* Complete (on paper or mentally) thoughts which begin with the words, "I should have done . . . " or "I wish I hadn't said . . . " or "If only I hadn't made that decision, I wouldn't . . . "

2. *What have others done to us that we are still refusing to let go of?* Make a list.

3. *Who is the single person you have the most difficulty with?* (As you are reading this, I am sure he/she has already come to mind.)

4. *What do you have to lose if you let yourself and the others off the hook?*

Forgiveness is a choice and a commitment. We can choose to hold onto our resentment toward mom and dad for what we perceive as their poor modeling, poor instruction, insensitivity to our needs, unfair attitudes and all the neurotic and unhealthy ideas, words and messages we learned. Or we can choose to see that they did the best they could under the circumstances, and within the framework of what they knew. We are old enough now to possess the insight and understanding necessary to change our family dynamics, so that we won't have to pass our own resentments on to our children, partners and friends. And we have to accept that we will face that choice everyday of our lives. We don't have to do it alone. We can get help.

It may not seem like we have this choice, but we do. It takes courage to dedicate ourselves to the process of forgiving. But once we cross the bridge, we'll never want to turn back again to our old life of resentment and retaliation.

Often we spend our entire lives searching for that special person who will forgive us, tell us that everything is okay, tell us we aren't a bad person. We search through books, attend classes, experiment with different religions all in the hope of learning how to let go of the negativity we no longer want to carry around inside. But we must come to see that forgiveness begins with a change of heart, a shift in how we see ourselves, our lives, our past and the people we met along the way.

Gerald Jampolsky described this attitude shift when he wrote:

> Forgiveness does not mean we must remarry our ex-spouse, let prisoners out of jail, return to our old job, or anything else overt. . . . Forgiveness is an inner correction that lightens the heart. . . . It is the relinquishing of an unhelpful train of thought. . . . Forgiveness is a gentle vision that sees the maturity, the goodness of heart, and the wholeness of character that will come to each person. And it recognizes the inappropriateness of condemnation to this growth process.

Forgiveness is the recognition and understanding that when we are retaliatory, vindictive, punishing, resentful and revengeful we become the victims of our own attitudes and actions. When I attack you, I attack myself. What I hold against you, I hold against myself. When I release you, I release myself as well. Vindictiveness is like an open sore which can only be healed if we take the necessary steps to prevent the infection from setting in. For many of us, such abscesses just keep on going deeper and deeper, affecting more and more areas of our life.

Forgiveness, therefore, is simply another word for acceptance. This means that despite what we've done in the past; despite the decisions we've made; despite all the mistakes we've made; despite all of the fears we have; despite the many things we want to change about ourself and our life . . . we are willing to begin the process of letting go of whatever separates us from accepting who and what we are and in accepting others for who they are. This doesn't mean that we must stay in destructive relationships. It does mean that as we open the doors to doing the things which foster self-love and self-respect, we will be empowered in making healthy decisions and changes.

All forgiveness asks of us is that we have the willingness or desire to live a more peaceful life. The moment we take the step to ask for help in letting go of the past, we have opened the door to our Higher Power . . . to the healing power of God's love.

Our Higher Self helps us to view life from a new and broadened perspective and assists us in the process of releasing whatever we are unable to release alone. All that is required is the willingness to ask. This is not to say that we deny our feelings or deny what happened. It does mean that we see the wisdom of not letting our past control us any longer.

Like the rest of you, I have had many important lessons to learn about forgiveness in my own life. I never knew what it really meant to forgive. My only experience of forgiveness was from my religious training and the lessons I learned from that experience taught me nothing. The fact is, if I hadn't learned what forgiveness means I would never have been able to let go of the attitudes which separated me from my father.

My dad and I had a difficult and strained relationship for the first twenty-eight years of my life. He attempted to prepare me for life by teaching me that "you can't trust anyone." He taught me about prejudice, and to be aware of the world's negative aspects. In trying to teach me the attitudes he thought necessary to survive, he showed me how to be angry, spiteful, intensely jealous, and how to be alone, and stay alone, in a very unfriendly world. He had no friends and didn't seem to trust anyone. Despite all this, my dad became my teacher of love and forgiveness. Even though my mother was very loving and devoted to her family and my two sisters and I were very close, my lessons really came from resolving my stormy relationship with my dad. How can you ignore someone who tears the door off the hinges when he gets angry and pounds his fist on the dining room table when he's making a point?

Basically, we disagreed on everything. He became very angry with me when I didn't see the world the same way he did. And so, we didn't communicate much and I spent very little time with him. He was a musician. When I got up in the morning to go to school, he was asleep. When I got home from school, he was getting ready to go to work. Our schedules were out of sync.

My dad was born in Louisiana and raised in Chicago. When he was a boy, World War I was underway. He was a pianist in the many clubs which surrounded the Chicago area during the 30's. He played in a club which had the distinction of being located next to where the St. Valentine Day massacre took place.

His mistrust, stubbornness, inflexibility, selfrighteousness, toughness and temper (which was on a par with a raging bull) were all qualities which were part of the times. He tried to teach me what he knew, what he had experienced in his lifetime. When I didn't seem to believe what he was sharing with me, he told me that I was young and didn't know better.

All in all, we weren't very close, we weren't very loving, we didn't have much to talk about. Then one day something happened: I decided not to try to change him. I refused to participate in the highly charged arguments centering on racism, mistrust, who was right and who was wrong. And when one person makes a decision not to participate in the unhealthy aspects of a relationship, the relationship changes.

A relationship, in one sense, is a chemical mixture of several ingredients. Sometimes the mixture is toxic. To avoid the toxicity I had to change the formula. Biting and provocative remarks were met with unresponsiveness. I changed the subject and talked about something healthier, like a project I was working on. I would ask him for his advice. He was an exceptionally gifted carpenter and enjoyed all kinds of woodwork. Woodwork provided a healthy connection between us. It was one of many healthy threads which together would develop the bonds between us.

Over the next few years, I found many areas in which we could share. He was an outstanding pianist and so I bought him classical recordings to listen to. Music became another point of contact. I began to see, as I turned 30 years old, that if I wanted to change our relationship, I had to change my perception of the relationship. If I only perceived our differences, the mixture was explosive. But if I concentrated on areas of connectedness, the mixture was homogenous.

I slowly began to put things into perspective. My father was raised in a very prejudiced era. He was a young and impressionable boy when racism was of epidemic proportions in this country. He joined a gang for self-protection and retaliation. He rubbed elbows with the gangsters of Chicago and played for many of their parties. I was trying to change him? How foolish. What needed change was how I related to him. I made a decision to see beyond and through all the roles, façades and illusions which I associated with him. I knew that there was a beautiful and loving person deep inside of him begging for expression. I now saw that his anger, his resentment, his vindictiveness, and his mistrust were a plea for help.

I forgave myself for all my years of arrogance and ignorance. I committed myself and our relationship to friendship and love. I found if my father refused to relate to me in a new and healthy way and insisted on continuing to be argumentative, then I would have to make a serious decision about whether to continue our relationship or, possibly, try to find another approach. I decided not to be concerned with that possibility. Why second guess myself, I thought, when I haven't even given the test a chance. I decided I'd cross that bridge if I came to it.

My father and I always greeted each other with a firm handshake. I decided to cup his hand with both of my hands to establish a healthy and warm physical greeting. From this, we slowly progressed to a handshake accompanied by me lovingly holding and touching his shoulder. The next step was a hug; once we hugged we never shook hands again. These transitions took years, but once the commitment was made, I never gave up.

Our relationship steadily improved. We began to openly acknowledge our love and concern for one another. We looked at each other with kindness and a deep respect. All was well.

Then it was discovered that he had cancer. The last two years of his life were the most painful I had ever experienced; for I deeply felt his suffering, his frustration, his disappointments. His first surgery removed one of his lungs. He recovered slowly but steadily, but he looked as if he had aged 10 years in a few months. He took a turn for the worse. The cancer had spread to his other lung. He was told he only had a short time to live. I was furious with the doctor for telling him that. When we were alone, my father cried and told me he might die. He hoped that the doctor was wrong.

My sister discovered an experimental program for eradicating the tumor with a lazer. My father underwent the surgery. He was also under the care of a nutritionist who altered his diet and supplemented his nutritional intake with high doses of vitamins. We all tried to encourage him with articles written by people who had fought cancer and who had won. He continued to lose weight.

I gave him literature on curing cancer through forming a relationship with the healing power of the Holy Spirit. I bought him a cassette player and some meditation tapes geared to reestablishing his relationship with God. He had a difficult time listening to the tapes and he didn't want to read the material.

I remember one very special day just before he died. He had a lot of back pain. I visited him at home and he told me of his discomfort and I told him I was an excellent masseur and wanted to rub his back. We went into the bedroom. He laid on the bed and I gently rubbed the muscles along his lower back. He told me that I had great hands. Looking down at him I was filled with love. Before I left he asked me if I would be willing to do one more thing for him; rub his back again. It was such a gift to be able to do it one more time. I was honored.

A few weeks later he was rushed to the hospital. His stomach burst open sending toxins into his system. I assisted in the intensive care room. He was fighting everyone in the room. He was speaking a language I couldn't understand. He was delusional. I assisted the staff in trying to hold him down on the table so that they could put him on the support systems. I tried calming him and attempted to bring some peace into the nightmare. My father was experiencing a toxic psychosis and I felt utterly helpless. He was hooked up to every machine imaginable. The staff was wonderful. They treated him with compassion, dignity and a lot of love. He was dying, he was in a lot of pain but he was in good hands. Thank God, I thought, he was here.

My family was called into the conference room with the attending physicians who told us he would have to undergo another surgery to close up the hole in his stomach. If they didn't operate, they said, he would be dead in a few hours. If they did operate, his chances were poor for surviving the surgery. Somehow he survived the surgery. When I visited him in the recovery room I was only able to recognize him because of his hair line. His face was all distorted and puffed up. I prayed for his recovery. We all did.

When I went to the hospital the following day, I asked the family if I could spend a few minutes with him alone. I placed my hands on his heart and adapted my breathing rhythm to his and concentrated on the love energy flowing from me to him. I asked him if he could hear me; he nodded yes. I asked him if he was in pain; he shook his head 'no.' I looked into his eyes, but we couldn't seem to establish eye contact. He seemed to be staring into space. I told him how much I loved him and how proud I was to be his son; how blessed I was to have him for my father. I stroked his head and stayed with him for a few minutes longer and letting all the love I felt for him flow forth. I touched his arms, his hands, his fingers, his chest, his shoulders, kissed him and said "goodbye for now." He died the next day.

I am so thankful that I took the necessary steps to get to know my father. If I hadn't initiated the healing of the rift between us, I never would have experienced the power of his love. There would have been so much unfinished business between us. Letting go of my misperceptions opened my eyes to his beauty and my heart to the well-spring of Love within him.

We all have so much to give to each other, so many insights to share and experiences to offer. Cynthia is a vibrant and sensitive woman who was on my staff at Ventura College for many years. She is incredibly gifted in working with both the developmentally disabled and the chronically mentally ill. She moved across the country to New York a few years ago with her two sons and within a few months of being there, her youngest son committed suicide. When I heard the tragic news I knew I wanted to share my experiences of my father's death with her. I knew the circumstances were quite different, but I also knew what it was to feel totally helpless in difficult circumstances and to blame myself and question whether I could have done something to prevent the death from happening. I knew what it was like to cry and feel the sorrow in losing a loved one who is an important part of one's life. I knew about the experiences I had after my father's death, seeming to contact him in my dreams, meditations and in a response to my prayers. These were the experiences I knew, and I shared them with her in a letter. It was a risk, an opening of myself to the possibility of rejection or misunderstanding. Here is what she wrote in reply:

Dear John:
I am apologizing for taking so much time to answer your letter. It meant so much to me. I especially appreciated the insights from your experiences at the time of your father's death. It was just too difficult for me to write to people for a while after my son's death. It still will be hard for a long time to come. It's all so irrevocable and difficult to understand.

I accepted your idea of trying to get in touch with him through prayer, meditation and intense concentration. Two very strange things happened. I've not shared this with very many people because I'm sure they would think me quite crazy, but I know you will understand.

One day when I was riding home with a friend I saw a vision [?] of him [her son] in the sky, dressed as he always was: jeans and a rock shirt. It was as if he was suspended there and he spoke to me, "I'm okay, Mom. I am here and I am happy. Please don't cry any more!" I felt a terrific sense of peace and relief. A few nights later I awoke from a sound sleep and heard the same message with the same result and fell into a deep, peaceful sleep for the first time in months. So strange, but it really helped me to cope.

My job has been a big help to me also. I really enjoy it and feel that I am really accomplishing some very positive things with it. It has been a Godsend for me. Anne and Janey sent me A Course in Miracles, and as I work my way through this, new ideas and thoughts help me clear my mind and give me direction in my life. I live alone now for

129

the first time in many years as my other son has moved on to make his own life. Even though we live in the same town and I see him frequently, things are quite different for me and every day is a challenge to try and get more out of life.

All best regards,
Cynthia

Most of the difficulties we experience in life have their origin in loss and separation; whether it be our present experience of it, the anticipation of it or the memory of it. In this process of forgiving, it's important that we get assistance in opening to our grief, our anger, and to all the emotions which loss and separation conjure up. As we begin to clear away all that prevents us from healing our relationship with ourself and others, our life will be transformed.

Forgiveness is an act of courage; for it requies courage to see beyond roles and expectations and to see ourself and our life in a new and healthier perspective.

A dear friend of mine, Margaret, aptly stated it when she said:

> "I am learning that forgiving is our natural heritage and anything that we attempt to do aside from this creates chaos within our souls. It seems that there is so much work for each of us to do in learning to open our hearts and to forgive ourselves and one another. With each step we take, the separation closes further until once again, we shall be One."

Do the things that you want to do ... things that ignite your life, give you power and a feeling of inner warmth. And stop doing the things which deaden you!

Bartholomew
I Come As A Brother

CHAPTER X

---

50 WAYS TO LOVE AND
BE LOVED

---

1. Recognize the things I do well and appreciate myself more and more each and every day.
2. Talk to myself gently, compassionately, and lovingly and catch myself in the midst of the critical self-talk.
3. Buy myself a huge bouquet of flowers. Plant flowers in the yard and play in the earth.
4. Clarify what I value and what is really important to me.
5. Allow the time for me to do the things I want to do.
6. Spend time with people whom I respect and who respect me.
7. Respect my needs and wants.
8. Set goals and organize a plan to accomplish them.
9. See the lesson in every 'so called' failure, disappointment or mistake. The question always is, "What can I learn from this?"
10. Never identify with the word 'failure.'
11. Learn to live in the present by cultivating an attitude of gratitude for all I have and for all the opportunities available to me.
12. Learn to identify the early warning signs of stress and find ways to relax and release my pent-up energy and emotions.

13. Focus on the positive not the negative; what I spend most of my time thinking about will manifest.
14. Uncover my inner resources. If there is a problem, there is an answer.
15. Laugh at myself often and see the absurdity of my melodrama.
16. Cultivate and nurture a sense of humor and a playful attitude.
17. Strive to live by and stand up for what I value and believe in.
18. Learn to say yes when I mean yes and no when I mean no!
19. Acknowledge when I don't know. Not knowing is really okay.
20. Allow time everyday to daydream, play, and to let my imagination run wild. Maybe I'll take an early morning walk, or write a poem, or watch the clouds float by, or dance around the house as I listen to some great music.
21. Pamper and indulge myself without feeling guilty about it. I can take myself to a movie, out to dinner, to a play, or buy myself a beautiful gift! And I can treat someone else!
22. See challenges where I once saw problems; choices and options where I once felt stuck.
23. Avoid all-or-nothing, black-and-white thinking; life is replete with color.
24. Let go of the 'should' and 'if only' beliefs and attitudes.
25. Surround myself with beauty and with things which vitalize and inspire me. The fact is, life is to be enjoyed!
26. Take risks, and do more of the things I love and want to do.
27. Seek and get help if I need it.
28. Meditate each and every day and ask for guidance,

inner clarity, a more loving attitude, patience, and a bright outlook.

29. Learn of the continuing power of using affirmations, smiling at myself in the mirror, and in visualizing myself in pleasurable circumstances with people I love and who love me.
30. Attend an ongoing support group or see a therapist to help me with the transitions and life changes I continue to make.
31. Listen more; there's a reason I have two ears and one mouth.
32. Follow the three injunctions: love myself; don't judge or criticize myself; don't compare myself to anyone else.
33. Accept who and what I am, even though I want to make many changes within and without. Self-acceptance is the path to peace of mind and to creating harmony in all my relationships.
34. Discover the wisdom of letting go of worn-out beliefs and attitudes.
35. Always remember: a difficult day is only 24 hours long. Tomorrow is a new day; tomorrow I can make another choice.
36. Use a journal to become more intimate with myself.
37. Treat myself like I would treat my dearest friend.
38. Discover more and more ways to express myself creatively, take an art or a dance class or sign up for something totally different and out of character.
39. Exercise regularly and take good care of my health needs.
40. Eat foods that energize me and lighten my step.
41. Forgive myself for all the perceived 'dumb' things I did or said and for all the things I didn't do.

42. Forgive myself for one more thing each day. I am the only one who can let myself off the hook; I'm the only one who can stop punishing myself.
43. Dare to dream, to stretch and to move beyond my current life script. If I can dream about it I can achieve it.
44. Write a letter to a friend I've been wanting to make contact with for a long time.
45. Challenge a fear that has stopped me from doing something I want to do.
46. Express myself clearly, honestly, and lovingly.
47. Choose to be happy for one full day.
48. Express the appreciation I feel for someone, whether it be through a letter, telephone call or by spending time together.
49. Accept a compliment and/or give one to someone else.
50. Find new and creative ways to love myself and others. The more I love myself, the more love I'll extend and receive.

AN AFFIRMATION

I have unlimited potential and freedom to love, learn, create, give, grow, and be happy. I am free to make decisions and to make choices which make my life fulfilling. I am free to establish priorities which reflect my own inner needs. I am free to be myself, free to play, free to smile, free to laugh. Free to enjoy this beautiful day, free to do the things which I love to do and to be with people whom I respect and who respect me. I am free to 'let go.' I have been created to love and to be loved and to live a life filled with joy, passion, excitement, adventure, and lots and lots of fun. I am developing a wonderul sense of humor and everyday learning the wisdom of laughing at myself, particularly when I take life so damn seriously. Each and every day I am smiling more and seeing the beauty within each person I meet and seeing my own beauty reflected there. My relationship with myself is growing and expanding. My single goal is peace of mind. My single goal is the peace of God.

REFERENCE

BIBLIOGRAPHY

CHAPTER I.

Caddy, Eileen *Foundations of Findhorn,* page 82. Findhorn Publications, 1978

Gorman, Paul and Ram Dass, *How Can I Help: Stories and Reflections on Service,* page 28. Alfred A Kropf, 1985.

Cox, Barbie, a selection from her poetry.

CHAPTER II.

Bach, Richard, *Illusions,* pages 6-10. Delacorte Press, 1977.

Block Lawrence, "Conquering the Ultimate Writer's Block." page 20, *Writer's Digest,* April 1984.

CHAPTER III

Castaneda, Carlos, *The Teachings of Don Juan,* page 105. Ballentine Books 1978. Block Lawrence, "Conquering the Ultimate Writer's Block," page 20, *Writers Digest.* April, 1984.

Dyer, Wayne, *Your Erroneous Zones,* page 91. Funk and Wagnalls, 1976.

Trine, Ralph Waldo, *In Tune with the Infinite,* page 79. The Bobbs-Merrill Co., 1908.

Frankel, Viktor, *Man's Search for Meaning,* pages 24 and 25. Pocket Books, 1963.

Washburn, Michael and Stark, Michael, *The Meeting of the Ways,* edited by John Welwood, page 79. Schoken Books, 1979.

Jung, C.G., *Memories, Dreams, Reflections,* page 325. Vintage Books, 1961.

Roszak, Theodore, *The Unfinished Animal,* Harper Colophon Books, 1971.

Ferguson, Marilyn, *The Aquarian Conspiracy,* page 198, Jeremy Tarcher, 1980.

Jampolsky, Gerald, *Love is Letting Go of Fear*, page 17. Bantam Books, 1981.

Castaneda, Carlos, *The Teachings of Don Juan*, page 79. Ballantine Books.

CHAPTER IV
Feild, Rashad, *There is Only to Be*, a cassette tape.

CHAPTER V
Moss, Richard, *The I That Is We*, page 28. Celestial Arts, 1981.

CHAPTER VI
Welwood, John, *Awakening the Heart*, page ix. Shambhala Books, 1983.
Tulku, Tarthank, *Gesture of Balance*, page 85. Dharma Publishing, 1972.
Moss, Richard. *The I That Is We*, page 25. Celestial Arts, 1981.
Easwaran, Eknath, *Meditation*, page 11. Blue Mountain Meditation Center, 1978.
Bragdon, Claude, *Delphic Woman*, page 140. Alfred Knopf Press, 1936.
Vaughn, Frances. *Awakening Intuition*, page 176. Anchor Books, 1979. Ibid.
Eliot, T.S. *Burnt Norton*, page 15. Harvest/HBJ, 1943.

CHAPTER VII
Ullmann, Liv, *Changing*, page 206. Alfred A. Knopf, 1977.

CHAPTER VIII
A *Course In Miracles*, page 105. Foundation for Inner Peace (text). Tiburon, Calif., 1975.

CHAPTER IX
Levine, Stephen, *Who Dies?*, pages 73-74. Anchor Books. 1982.
Jampolsky, Gerald, *Teach Only Love*, pages 110-112. Bantam Books, 1983.

CHAPTER X
Bartholomew, *I Come As A Brother*, page 42. High Mesa Press, 1986.

ABOUT THE AUTHOR

photo by Morgan Rudolph

Dr. John A. Tamiazzo has been teaching classes on The Transforming Power of Love for Santa Barbara City College Adult Education, Psychology, and Personal Development Department, since 1983. He lectures regularly throughout Southern California and has been a frequent guest speaker on television, talk radio, and for many Human Service Organizations. He offers intensive workshops on Love, Intimacy, Self-Esteem, and the integration of Clinical Hypnosis and Dream Therapy, as well as classes in Transpersonal and Humanistic Psychology.

If you wish to order an autographed copy of LOVE AND BE LOVED, please include a check or money order with the order form below. Make checks payable to John A. Tamiazzo, Ph.D., and send to Post Office Box 91339, Santa Barbara, CA 93190-1339.

Name _____

Address _____

City _____ State _____ Zip _____

_____ books @ $9.95 $ _____

Shipping/handling $1.25

Calif. sales tax 6% $ _____
Please allow   (if applicable)
1–2 weeks
for delivery.   TOTAL $ _____

Also available From John A. Tamiazzo is a beautiful 90-minute cassette tape with excerpts from LOVE AND BE LOVED. Please send check or money order with the order form below.

Name _____

Address _____

City _____ State _____ Zip _____

_____ cassettes @ $9.95 $ _____

Subtotal $ _____

Shipping/handling $1.00

Calif. sales tax 6% $ _____
Please allow   (if applicable)
1–2 weeks
for delivery.   TOTAL $ _____